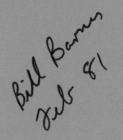

Bill Barnes
Feb 81

Footsteps in the Sea

Footsteps in the Sea

Roy C. Nichols

Abingdon / Nashville

FOOTSTEPS IN THE SEA

Copyright © 1980 by Abingdon

Library of Congress Cataloging in Publication Data

NICHOLS ROY C, 1918-
  Footsteps in the sea.
  1. Sermons, American. 2. Methodist Church— Sermons. I. Title.
  BX833.N48F66   252'.076   79-26826

ISBN 0-687-13270-3

MANUFACTURED BY THE PARTHENON PRESS
NASHVILLE, TENNESSEE, UNITED STATES OF AMERICA

To my wife, Ruth,
whose careful concern for Melisande, Allegra,
Nathan, and me, has enriched our lives.

Contents

Preface

Good religion bridges all the disconnections that threaten to partition segments of our common life into unrelated zones of thought and action. *Footsteps in the Sea* affirms the presence, power, and pervasive relevance of the One God, whose Holy Spirit crisscrosses all human history and every human circumstance.

Jesus is presented herein as the incarnate witness of the One God; the spiritual Son of God, revealed in flesh, whose words and deeds incited the beginnings of the Christian covenantal community. This understanding does not preclude the universal influence of what John Wesley called prevenient grace; nor the awareness of the omnipresent revelation of God in the whole creation.

It is my hope that all who take the time to share these thoughts will find a blessing.

Roy C. Nichols
Pittsburgh, Pennsylvania

Chapter I

God Moves
Genesis 1:1-2

Two children sat before a desert campfire in a Bedouin family circle, thousands of years ago. They were gazing at a full moon, awestruck by the singular brilliance of this great heavenly body. It seemed that darkness had been turned into day. Suddenly, the little girl asked her aging grandfather, who was sitting close by, "What is that great light?" A little boy added his question, "And where did it come from?"

The old man, with a twinkle in his eye, began to unfold slowly the story that had been passed on to him through many generations. With practiced poise, he began: "Before God created the heavens and the earth everything was dark and jumbled. So, before God could begin the task of putting everything in order, God made two great lights, the greater light to shine during the day and the lesser light to shine at night. You've seen the sun at midday," the old man said, "and that is the moon above us tonight."

The children nodded attentively. "God made the sun and the moon," said the little girl, "so he could see."

I remember the first time I beheld the magnificence of the moon. My sisters and I were spending the summer on the farm with our grandparents on the eastern shore of Maryland. I was about eight years old. One night, after twisting and turning in bed with a minor stomachache, I awoke. My eye caught sight of a beam of light flooding through the window like a great searchlight, spreading its radiance on the wooden floor. At first I was frightened. Then slowly I slipped out of the bed and quietly tiptoed toward the open window. First, I looked straight ahead, then upward. There it was—a big, round, bright ball! The tasseled corn in the field below was aglow. The darkened wooded areas looked ominous. Long shadows of tall trees sketched eerie silhouettes on the ground. It was an indescribable moment of silent awe for me.

During the winter months we lived in Philadelphia. I had seen the moon before, but always against the competing glare of city lights. I had never beheld the moon in such splendor. Quietly I made my way back to the bed. My midnight discovery was a secret. Like most children I plunged into the activities of a new day and forgot the moon's wonderment. But through the years, that special moment of awe and mystery continued in my memory. Long before I understood the astronomy of the heavenly bodies, that moonlight revelation and subsequent manifestations of nature prepared me for a deeper understanding of the marvelous handiwork of God.

Almost twenty years ago, when President Kennedy announced the American moon venture, the reaction was mixed. Some people applauded the prospect of this demonstration of American superiority. But there were others who did not think such an achievement possible. Some dubbed it an insolent human invasion of divine privacy. Still others felt that such a mission might disturb the rhythm of the heavenly bodies. But in 1969 Neil Armstrong transformed fiction into fact and landed on the moon. This amazing accomplishment has increased rather than diminished our sense of the vastness of the universe. The more we learn, the more we are aware of the limitless mystery of the unknown.

Space explorations, above all else, have confirmed the fact that the universe is composed of an orderly and dependable arrangement of objects and occurrences. Einstein once characterized all scientific research as "divine inquiry." Science is the act of seeking to know, to understand, and to use the marvelous capacities of the human mind to apply and appropriate the resources of the universe in new and creative ways.

Science and religion are two parts of the same pursuit. Any attempt to separate them is detrimental to both. God's revelation is apparent in the test tube, the telescope, and geological and medical research, as well as in Scripture, reason, tradition, and experience. The Latin infinitive from which the word "science" is deprived is *scire,* which means, "to know." The word "religion," on the other hand, is rooted in the Latin infinitive *religare,* which means, "to bind" or "to bring together." Good religion increases our awareness of the relationships which unite the whole of creation.

Our understanding of the nature of God will always be proscribed if our thought forms are separated into secular and sacred dominions. The dogmatism of medieval religion was partially responsible for the broken linkage between science and theology. The church refused to alter its traditional opinions regarding the composition of the universe, so scientists declared their independence in order to pursue the search for truth unbridled by restrictions imposed by the hierarchy. There is one God and one truth. Though we may approach the truth on different paths, the common objective is the same.

Science is the practical pursuit of knowledge. Theology is the search for meaning. Science, depending upon its confirmed researches, exclaims, "Look what we have discovered." Religion, with equal gusto, declares, "Look what we perceive." To perceive is to be aware of a larger truth, beyond our present human ability to completely describe, comprehend, or verify. Theology begins where science begins, but it continues its truth—seeking journey beyond the scientific domain.

If a theologian had accompanied Armstrong to the moon, awestruck by the spectacle of space and space objects, he or she might well have joined the psalmist in saying: "The heavens declare the glory of God; and the firmament showeth his handiwork. Day unto day uttereth speech, and night unto night showeth knowledge" (Psalm 19:1-2). William Cowper, writing in the eighteenth century, wrote some words of poetry found in the hymnbook of almost every church: "God moves in a mysterious way / His wonders to perform; / He plants his footsteps in the sea, / and rides upon the storm."

The book of Genesis describes a God who moves. God speaks and things begin to happen; the heaven and earth appear. Water and light follow. Then, in response to the spoken word, vegetation, trees, the seasons, plants, and the constellations take form. God calls fish and fowl into being. Creeping things and beasts appear. God said that everything was "good." Then, reflecting on all that had been created, God said that it was "very good" (Genesis 1:1 ff.).

James Weldon Johnson, in his remarkable poem entitled "The Creation," describes the movement of God in a most interesting fashion. God strides across the face of the earth, hollowing the valleys and forcing the upward thrust of mountains.

And God walked, and where He trod,
His footsteps hollowed the valleys out
And buldged the mountains up.

What a fascinating way to depict the creative movements of God. The verified evolutionary findings of the scientist add to the credibility of the Bible. For "a day," described in the book of Genesis, might have been a thousand years of milleniums. Science attempts to explain how it all happened. The Bible declares why it all happened.

Dr. Robert Jastrow, a nationally known NASA space scientist, describes the begining of creation thus:

> According to astronomical evidence our universe was created twenty billion years ago in a shattering explosion. . . . The world prior to that time was a black and formless void. . . . The scientist can never hope to discover whether the agent of creation was the personal God of the Old Testament or one of the familiar forces of physics, for the searing blast of that first moment has erased the fingerprints of the prime mover."

Scientists call this the "big bang theory." The Bible simply says, "God spoke." The all-powerful word of God was the first cause.

According to the account in the book of Genesis, God's most significant move ocurred when the Creator stooped to make the human form from the dust of the earth. Then God breathed divine life into that human being and "man became a living soul." In summarizing the biblical account, the author of Genesis says, "So God created man in his own image, . . . male and female created he them" (1:26-27). The God of the Bible is not a remote and distant being. God is the infinite, immediate presence and power, creating and sustaining. God moves and is involved continually in the details of creation, history, and the individual life of every creature; and especially in the experience of human beings. So we who profess faith in God declare that God not only exists but that God is relevant to everything that ever has been, is, and will be. But even more important, God has a careful concern for the life and experience of each human being.

Dr. George Washington Carver, the brilliant botanist from Tuskegee University, was described as "The man who talked with the flowers." But Carver's conversations were not prompted by an animistic belief that God resided in the petals of a rose. Rather, he saw the miracle of God's handiwork reflected in every natural phenomenon. So he found spiritual edifiction as he spoke to and through the flowers words of inquiry and concern addressed finally to nature's God.

Karl Marx, the man who has shaken the foundations of the nineteenth and twentieth centuries, characterized religion as the "opiate of the people." His view of the nineteenth-century European church led him to believe that religious leaders had actually contributed to the oppression of the poor by collaborating with the rich. Furthermore, Marx believed that religion tended to teach people to accept passively their poverty and oppression in the expectation of heavenly rewards after death while the religious instructors of the poor lived in lavish luxury. The revolutionary consequences of Marxism were a judgment on the unholy state-church alliances of Europe, the Middle East and Russia. But the atheist who quarantines himself or herself against God because of the abuses of religious power or quarrels with institutional religion imprisons his or her own spiritual possibilities. Such isolation prevents that extraordinary experience of liberty which reaches beyond all human confinements toward a hope which refuses to accept any human success as a final victory or any human failure as a final defeat.

A little boy was working with his father in a backyard garden. They were preparing the ground for planting. The lad was trying to move a rock from the flower bed. He tugged and tugged at it unsuccessfully. Finally, exhausted, he said, "I can't do it." His father, looking on, said, "But you haven't used all your strength." The little boy squatted again and pulled with all his might. Then, looking toward his father, he expressed his frustration all over again. Smiling, the father responded, "But you haven't used all your strength. . . . You haven't asked me to help you." Then the father and the son tugged at the rock together. It moved. Faith supplements all the earthly strength we possess. It reaches above and beyond our human resources. Faith refuses to be defeated by human frailties. It is an attitude toward the universe which continually expects the aid of the infinite resourcefulness of nature's God.

The New Testament account of the life and work of Jesus of Nazareth is the story of a unique act of divine revelation. St. Paul, in his famous Mars' Hill sermon to the intellectuals of ancient Greece, declared that the God of the whole universe revealed a divine message to the whole creation in Jesus Christ. God was in Christ, the great apostle went on to say, "Reconciling the world unto himself" (II Corinthians 5:19). John's Gospel describes Jesus as the "word" of God made flesh. "Word" is the English translation of the Greek word *logos,* "the expression or meaning."

The early church fathers attempted to transmit to future generations the marvelous fact of the Incarnation and their understanding of the indwelling presence of the

Holy Spirit in the Christian trinitarian theological formulation. The doctrine of the Trinity, the God who is three in one, is an effort to express the triune manifestations of the one God who is continually involved in the process of creation and recreation. So they declared God to be Father, Son, and Holy Ghost.

Bishop Paul L. A. Granadosin, of the United Methodist Church in the Philippines, introduced me to the wording of a hymn used in congregational singing in the Filipino churches. In a most exciting way the poet speaks of the wonders of the God who is integral to our contemporary technological civilization:

> God of concrete, God of steel,
> God of piston and of wheel,
> God of nylon, God of steam,
> God of girder and of beam,
> God of atom, God of mind;
> All the world of power is thine.
>
> Lord of cable, Lord of rail,
> Lord of freeway and of mail,
> Lord of rocket, Lord of flight,
> Lord of roaring satellite,
> Lord of lightning's flashing blind,
> All the world of speed is thine.
>
> Lord of science, Lord of art,
> Lord of map and graph and chart,
> Lord of physics and research,
> Lord of Bible, faith and church,
> Lord of sequence and design,
> All the world of truth is thine.
>
> God whose glory fills the earth,
> Gave the universe its birth,
> Charges men to re-create,

Love of God we celebrate,
Claims mankind by grace divine,
All the world of Life is thine.

In Christ this God becomes demonstrably clear in word
and deed, expounding the truth explicitly, with a
brilliance more dazzling than the noonday sun or the
radiant awesomeness of the full moon on a clear night.

Chapter II

I've Got Shoes
Exodus 2:11–3:14

✗ In the economy of the southern plantation, shoes were a precious possession to be worn on special occasions. For some, however, the price of a pair of shoes was out of reach. So a sensitive songster, anticipating that heaven would provide all things needful, put to words and music this blissful expectation:

> I've got shoes,
> You've got shoes,
> All God's children got shoes,
> When I get to heaven
> I'm going to put on my shoes,
> I'm going to walk all over God's heaven.

There is an Old Testament story about shoes. It centers around the experience of a man named Moses, the father of Jewish freedom. The epic of his leadership is well-known. He came to prominence during the time that Israel was enslaved in Egypt. He was adopted by Pharaoh's daughter and grew up in Pharaoh's court. One day Moses saw an Egyptian taskmaster beating a Jewish laborer with a bullwhip. Unable to repress his anger, Moses intervened and seized the foreman's whip. The foreman struck back. The two men, locked in fierce combat, fell to the ground. The Egyptian's head hit a rock. Suddenly he relaxed his grip and rolled over motionless. Minutes later, he breathed a rasping breath and died. Moses was frightened. With the help of the Hebrew he befriended, Moses dragged the Egyptian's body to an obscure place and buried it secretly. But when he discovered his deed was known, fearing Pharaoh's wrath, he fled into the wilderness and joined himself to the household of Jethro and became a herdsman in the nearby land of Midian (Exodus 2:11-25).

One day at dusk, as Moses herded his flock toward a sheltered place for the night, he saw a blazing bush. After securing his cattle, he turned toward the flame. He had not seen this strange spectacle before. As he drew near, suddenly he heard a voice calling him by name. Startled and fearful, his trembling voice responded, "Here am I."

Then, the voice of the Lord called out unto Moses, saying, "Put off thy shoes . . . for the place on which you are standing is holy ground." So Moses slowly stooped, with eyes still fixed on the dazzling fire, loosened his sandals and kicked them from his feet. Then kneeling, with his hands covering his face, he inquired, "What is thy name?" And the voice of the Lord responded, "I AM THAT I AM." That strange encounter was the turning point in the life of Moses and the history of his people. "Put off thy shoes" were words Moses never forgot.

Shoes were designed to protect the feet from the rough rigors of the road. But there are times when bare feet are a blessing; for example, walking on soft dirt in the summer; striding through stimulating granules of a sandy beach; exposing chilled feet before an open fire . . . or a burning bush. There is always the danger that the elaborate support systems of science and technology

which cushion our lives may insulate us so securely that all
our thoughts, feelings, and expressions will reflect only a
secondary muted awareness of the power and presence of
God.

In the Hollywood movie *O God,* the interesting
thought is introduced that the reason God created Adam
and Eve and gave them no clothes to wear was because
God knew that as soon as they had clothes they'd want
pockets. And as soon as they had pockets, they'd want
money. And as soon as they got money, there would be
trouble. For "the love of money is the root of all evil."
Money, which makes possible so many helpful things, can
be a barrier to spiritual understanding. Children who
grow up in cities, for example, must be carefully taught,
or their praise will go to the supermarket, the mall, and
money for all of their blessings. In the midst of Western
affluence, it is easy to become a worshiper of material
things, glorifying the creature rather than the Creator.

Francois Fénelon, the seventeenth-century French
mystic, once said, "The wind of God is always blowing;
but we must hoist our sails." Every person, if the meaning
of one's life is to achieve clarity and purpose, needs to
hear the voice of God, feel God's presence, experience
God's power. Prayer is the act of taking off one's shoes,
turning the eye and the ear of the soul toward the burning
bush. It is responding to God and speaking to God. It is
lifting the sails of our humanity to the wind of God.
Prayer is the divine connection. Like milk, vegetables and
meat, prayer is a natural. It is the breathing action of the
soul. This is why St. Paul directs us to "Pray without
ceasing" (I Thessalonians 5:17). Pray in order to stay
alive. The momentous confrontation at the burning bush
was for Moses the beginning of a new life of prayer, faith,

and good works as he struggled every step of the way to understand and respond to the will of God.

To speak of prayer frightens some people. It sounds like a retreat from reality, an effort to "let God do it" rather than doing our fair share of the world's work. St. Augustine of Hippo, the fourth-century African saint, gave timeless advice when he said, "No person should be so involved in the service of one's neighbor as to neglect the contemplation of God." But he was quick to add that no person should be so involved in the prayerful contemplation as to neglect one's service to one's neighbor. Prayer is for activists. For the God in whom we trust is a God who is on the move. Now, there are some serious risks in prayer, one might receive some dangerous direction from God. Certainly, Moses was distressed when the voice from the burning bush told him that he should return to Egypt to confront Pharaoh over the issue of the freedom of his people. He questioned God, saying, "Who am I, that I should go unto Pharaoh?" At times, we have all had the inspiration to make some brave witness or take some unpopular stand. But somewhere between the point of inspiration and the place where we were to articulate the message, we lost courage and fell silent.

A little girl was playing on the floor while her preacher father was busily writing out his sermon. "Daddy," the little girl inquired, "does God tell you what to say?" Thoughtfully, her father responded, "Yes." "Then," inquired the little girl, "why do you cross out so much?"

There are ancient and modern gurus who insist that God can only be perceived in quietness. So they cultivate the art of silence in retreat. But such a prayer style is only a partial description of a total prayer life. St. Paul describes the life of a true believer by using highly activized illustrations. In Ephesians we are wrestlers; in Timothy warriors; in Hebrews we are long-distance runners. Modern Christians will need to do most of their praying with their eyes wide open striding down the open road!

Some years ago Dr. Howard Thurman, one-time dean of the chapel at Boston University, introduced me to a prayer couplet I have continued to build upon: "O God, I need thee" and "O God, I thank thee." I liked his suggestion because it was geared to action. It did not require either preparation or isolation to be effective. I do my best praying when I'm moving—driving my car, or riding on a bus, grappling with a difficult problem, or enjoying a time of great exhiliration.

The first appeal is "O God, I need thee." Psalm 42 compares a thirsty deer searching for water to the soul in search of God. Our needs are too numerous to list on every occasion of prayer. Furthermore, St. Paul reminds us that "we know not what we should pray." Our dependence is placed upon the intercession of the Holy Spirit, who translates our insufficient language to God "with groanings which cannot be uttered" (Romans 3:26). To know that God understands the depth of needs you cannot properly describe relieves the prayer experience of anxiety and breathes a sense of security and strength.

The second prayer attitude is expressed in the words: "O God, I thank thee." Psalm 107 reads: "O give thanks unto the Lord for he is good; for his mercy endureth forever." These words may not always come easily. Hardship, illness, disappointment, and death are realities we all confront. But if we are able to accept our undeserved troubles with the same grace we accept our undeserved blessings, an amazing transformation can pervade our personalities. Genuine joy is the inheritance of the grateful life. This is not an endorsement of Pollyana artificiality, but an invitation to a life of barefoot realism that faces every burning bush listening for the voice of God.

For years my prayer life embraced just the two attitudes: "O God, I need thee" and "O God, I thank thee." But over a period of years a third and fourth prayer dimension entered my experience, completing the divine quatrain. At first, the third ingredient seemed superfluous: "O God, I love thee." Then, one day, with great seriousness, I found myself reflecting on the content of Psalm 116: "I love the Lord, because he hath heard my voice and my supplications." It suddenly dawned upon me how fortunate I was to have the benefit of a heavenly listener capable of meeting every need. The realization struck me with a flood of joy. The true believer finds a whole new channel of expression in the open confession of love for God.

Love replaces fear. Martin Luther, the sixteenth-century Protestant reformer, discovered that. After reading the fifth chapter of Romans, in which he perceived that God's love for us is a gift, Luther's fear of God's wrath and judgment gave way to an attitude of responsive love. Love transforms relationships between God and us.

In the world of human love relationships there comes a time when nothing can replace the spoken word. Gifts, tokens of affection, warm embraces still leave something lacking until the words are spoken: "I love you." These are the most powerful words on earth when uttered with conviction and sealed with unconditional commitment. So I have come to believe that God, who needs nothing, provides for each of us a divine opportunity, a chance to say the words: "O God, I love thee"—a manifestation of our warm respect for the one in whom "we live, and move, and have our being." On occasion, I find myself returning to the question which Jesus put so pointedly to Simon Peter: "Lovest thou me more than these?" Peter's response has more meaning to me now: ". . . I love thee."

The fourth prayer attitude is the one direct request in the fourfold petition of the heavenly jogger: "O God, make me a blessing." This is not a request that we be blessed, but that our lives may be a blessing to others. It is an announcement to God that we are available and that, furthermore, we desperately desire that God may put our lives to unselfish uses. There is a hymn by C. D. Meigs that expresses this meaning well:

> Lord, help me live from day to day
> In such a self-forgetful way
> That even when I kneel and pray
> My prayer will be for others.

Toyohiko Kagawa, the Japanese Christian who worked miracles in the slums of Kobe, Japan, witnessed through a life of service the love and grace of God. In his *Songs from the Slums* (Nashville: Cokesbury, 1935, p. 66) He says:

> I cannot invent
> New things,
> Like the airships
> Which sail
> On silver wings;
> But today
> A wonderful thought
> In the dawn was given . . .
> And the thought
> Was this:
> That a secret plan

I cannot invent
That my hand is big,
Big,
Because of this plan
That God,
Who dwells in my hand,
Knows the secret plan
Of the things he will do for the world
Using my hand!

A little boy attended a symphony concert with his parents. He was intrigued by the music, the instruments, and the movements of the artists. But most of all he enjoyed the man in the back row of the orchestra, with two great metal cymbals strapped to his wrists. Every now and then the man would rise and slam the cymbals together joyously, producing a resounding noise. After the concert the little boy's parents took him backstage to meet some of the musicians. Finally, he saw the man who played the cymbals. "What do you have to know to play the cymbals?" the little boy inquired. The man responded thoughtfully, "Nothing . . . except when!"

People often ask the same question about prayer. When do you pray? How do you pray? For what should we pray? The answer is—all that you need to know is "when"! When you are ready to put off your shoes, when you are ready to be honest with God, when you are prepared to respond to the voice from the burning bush, then you have all of the preparation that is required for a meaningful prayer life.

"Put off thy shoes . . ."

Chapter III

"Promises . . . Promises"
Genesis 12:1-2

Long, long ago, in upper Mesopotamia, in the region of Haran, there lived a man by the name of Abram. One day when Abram was walking alone, he heard the voice of the Lord saying: "Get thee out of thy country, and from thy kindred . . . unto a land that I will show thee: And I will make of thee a great nation, and I will bless thee, and make thy name great; and thou shalt be a blessing." So Abram gathered together his possessions, his family and kin and traveled northwest toward the Mediterranean Sea and settled in the land of Canaan.

In biblical history God's promise and Abram's response are interpreted to be a covenant relationship. A covenant in this sense is a holy transaction, initiated by God, in which promises are given and received. It makes possible a new human understanding of the will of God, inspiring binding commitment and establishing a trust relationship with divine sanction. Later in their history, Moses provided Abram's offspring with the Ten Commandments of God. Any thought or act which violated that law was considered a sin. In order to alleviate the burden of guilt and the prospect of punishment, an order of priestly mediators evolved. Animal sacrifices were used as substitute peace offerings to satisfy the covenantal requirements of the holy God.

The word "testament" and "covenant" have the same meaning. In biblical usage, the Old Testament is the old covenant; the New Testament is the new covenant. In the Epistle to the Hebrews, Christ is described as inaugurating a new covenant. He is, by divine initiative, the one who provides the all-sufficient sacrifice and offering for the sins of the whole world, replacing all that has gone before and nullifying the need for any future sacrifices. The author of Hebrews, referring to the old covenant in contrast to the blessings of the new covenant, says:

> "For if the blood of bulls and of goats, and the ashes of an heifer . . . sanctifieth . . . how much more shall the blood of Christ, who through the eternal Spirit offered himself without spot to God, purge your conscience from dead works to serve the living God? And for this cause he is the mediator of the new testament. . . . (Hebrews 9:13-15)

Jesus, who is the incarnate presence of God, therefore makes possible for all persons, and especially those who freely receive the gift, salvation.

It is difficult for twentieth-century sophisticates to appreciate or understand fully the enthusiasm with which this message was received in the first century. Before the coming of Christ, people were burdened with an overbearing sense of guilt and were captive to a sacramental system which required more from the poor than they could afford. Then, suddenly, in Christ, all persons are offered a new and living way. "Wherefore remember," says St. Paul, "that ye being in time past Gentiles in the flesh . . . [were] aliens from the commonwealth of Israel, and strangers from the covenants of promise, having no hope, and without God in the world: But now, in Christ Jesus, ye who sometimes were far off are made nigh by the blood of Christ. For he is our peace, who hath made both one, and hath broken down the middle wall of partition . . ." (Ephesians 2:11-14).

Jesus is the new point of convergence for Jew and Gentile, slave and free person, rich and poor, male and female. Christ makes possible the birth of a new race which includes all races; a new nation which includes all nations. Eusebius, the ancient ecclesiastical historian, indicates that the early Christians referred to themselves as "the new race" and "the new nation." This is clearly evident in the First Epistle of Peter: "Ye are a chosen generation, a royal priesthood, an holy nation, a peculiar people; that ye should show forth the praises of him who hath called you out of darkness into his marvelous light . . ." (2:9-10). Under the new covenant God is no longer a distant judge, separated from us by a high barrier of legalism, hierarchy, and ritual.

Covenants are common in the human situation; some are restrictive, others are inclusive. Without covenantal promises, mutually given and received, a society of persons has no trustworthy foundation. For example, the Pledge of Allegiance to the flag "and to the republic for which it stands, one nation under God, indivisible, with liberty and justice for all" is a covenantal transaction, making possible the establishment of a government "of the people, by the people, and for the people." A heterogeneous community of mixed cultures and races like the United States of America cannot survive unless that pledge is a deep commitment in the lives of the citizens of the nation. Our common pledge to the basic promises in the Constitution and the consideration of "equal justice" and "due process" is a profound statement of political mutuality, indispensable to the cohesion of this nation.

Covenant-keeping of this sort requires more than human sanction to succeed. Truly, the nation must conceive itself to be under the guidance of God, subjecting all of its decisions to the highest moral and ethical insights at our disposal. Abraham Lincoln, in one of his Thanksgiving messages to the nation, spoke words of deep concern which have a contemporary ring:

> We have forgotten the gracious hand which preserved us in peace and multiplied and enriched and strengthened us, and we have vainly imagined, in the deceitfulness of our hearts, that all these things were produced by some superior wisdom and virtue of our own . . . intoxicated with unbroken success, we have become too self-sufficient to feel the necessity of redeeming and preserving grace, too proud to pray to the God who made us.

Lincoln's emphasis here is not an appeal to a privatized piety, but rather to a public spirit of humility, acknowledging that the special prophecy in this nation cannot be fulfilled without a high level of covenantal commitment under God.

On a recent trip to Singapore, I saw 2,000 students standing to make their pledge to this tiny Far Eastern state. It was a moving experience to hear the echo of phrases inspired by our own Pledge of Allegiance: "We, the citizens of Singapore, pledge ourselves as one united people, regardless of race, language, or religion, to build a democratic society based on justice and equality, so as to achieve happiness, prosperity, and progress for our nation."

When two lovers present themselves for union in the sacred bond of marriage, they enter a profound covenantal relationship, pledging themselves, under God, to each other . . . "to have and to hold, from this day forward, for better, for worse, for richer, for poorer, in sickness and in health, to love and to cherish, till death us do part, according to God's holy ordinance . . ." Uncommitted living-together arrangements will never replace these solemn promises, which bespeak an unconditional oath to love and work for the mutual advantage of each other and of their offspring "till death us do part . . ."

When two baseball teams take the field, the contest between them is governed by a set of rules, understood and agreed upon by each player. A corps of umpires oversees the contest and makes critical decisions to keep the game honest. The final credibility of the game depends upon the faithfulness of all participants.

Human covenants involving persons and property are always reinforced by the prospect of legal penalties in case of default. But the divine covenant is initiated and received without coercion. The love-inspired promises of God incite a desire to please. St. Paul expresses that feeling well when he says, "Having therefore these promises (of God), dearly beloved, let us cleanse ourselves from all filthiness of the flesh and spirit, perfecting holiness in the fear of God" (II Corinthians 7:1). When a divinely inspired covenantal expression of God's love invades a life, there develops a spontaneous inclination to please God and to do God's will.

In chapter 10 of Hebrews there is a fourfold expression in the life of the true believer which is essential to the mission of the local church. The first is to share the good news of the truth of the gospel with everyone we meet. Blessings received cannot be kept secret. Truth must be declared and proclaimed. Evangelism, then, is the first fruit of the new covenant. The individual Christian and the whole church reach out to share the promise of God received in Jesus Christ.

Secondly, we rejoice in the opportunity to use our lives to inspire and arouse God's love in the lives of others. Contagious Christianity can precipitate a love epidemic. Thirdly, we look for the opportunity to engage the energy of our lives in redeeming deeds, which contribute to the liberation of persons and systems. And fourthly, the author of Hebrews insists that the covenantal people of God must come together for worship and mutual encouragement and to nurture their common hope of the kingdom of God. The local church, the place where Christian covenanters come together, is indispensable to the nurture and development of faith and good works in the lives of believers.

Divine covenant keeping, according to Martin Buber, is placing our lives under the control of God. It is a voluntary act of dedication in which we yield our separate intentions to a common purpose. This profound experience of divine/human mutuality makes us co-workers with God and joint heirs with Jesus Christ.

The true church of Jesus Christ can never be adequately described in pluralistic terms. John Wesley, the founding father of Methodism, once said, "As to all opinions which do not strike at the root of Christianity, we Methodists think and let think." But Mr. Wesley never intended, I am sure, to endorse the popular brand of poorly defined pluralism which punctures the covenantal relationship. The endorsement of optional lifestyles inconsistent with the teaching of Scripture, the dictates of reason, the testimony of credible tradition, and experience are out of order among the people of God! The consequence of covenanting closes the door on privatized situational preferences and the permissiveness of "consenting adults." Rather, we are bound by our promises to each other and to God.

Yoked together in the covenantal harness, we are no longer free to discriminate against other persons because of their race, sex, creed, or color. We have lost the liberty to decide what is right and what is wrong on the basis of situational convenience. We can no longer spend our money as we selfishly choose, since we are stewards. Our political and economic views are now under spiritual surveillance. And our private and public attitudes are on divine review.

Let us, therefore, joyfully bear the burden of Christ's discipleship in the world, laying aside every encumbrance, looking unto Jesus, who is the author and finisher of our faith.

John Wesley's covenantal prayer appropriately summarizes the intention of the faithful:

> I am no longer my own, but thine. Put me to what thou wilt, rank me with whom thou wilt; put me to doing, put me to suffering; let me be employed for thee or laid aside for thee, exalted for thee or brought low for thee; let me be full, let me be empty; let me have all things, let me have nothing; I freely and heartily yield all things to thy pleasure and disposal. . . .

Chapter IV

Male and Female
Genesis 1:26-28

With unmistakable clarity the Bible describes the creation of man and woman as a special act of God. The man and woman were formed separately, each with distinct characteristics but of the same substance. Scientific research has yet to explain precisely how human beings came to be. Similarity of structure and design with lower forms of life is evident, but the "missing link" between human beings and other species has not been found. Likewise, the marvelous composition of the human creature is without an equal in the whole of the known created universe. Anticipated interplanetary excursions may yet reveal unique forms of life, but so far outer space explorations tend to confirm the extraordinary uniqueness of the planet earth and the still expanding splendor of its highest form of life—*Homo Sapiens.*

Today the form and function of the sexes is a matter of considerable discussion. Traditional relationships between men and women are being challenged. At issue is the question of equality. The serious nature of the inquiry takes the form of the pertinent questions. Are men and woman equal? If so, in what sense are they equals? If not, why not? Much of the content of the Bible came through inspired men with strong paternalistic preoccupations. In the ancient world, women were considered the second order of creation and men the first.

Before the advent of technology and all of the conveniences associated with city living, physical strength was one of the first essentials for survival. Men hunted wildlife in the fields and forests. Men fought the battles to defend their clan and village against marauders. Women bore children, made the clothes, prepared the food, and cared for other domestic details. Women were incapacitated during intervals of childbearing; and, because the physical form and function of the female body makes women less strong, stereotypes of female inferiority became entrenched. But beyond this, in the Hebrew tradition, there was the notion that because Eve inspired the disastrous apple transaction in the garden, as recorded in Genesis account, she was responsible for original sin and its consequences for mankind. All of this has served to justify patterns of female repression.

A story is told of a little girl who spent the day playing with a little boy who kept telling her that little boys were better than little girls. That night the little girl knelt down for prayer, her mind perplexed by the memory of the overbearing taunts of her little male playmate. She followed her routine prayer with these words: "Dear God, are little boys really better than little girls?" After a brief pause, as if waiting for an answer, she added, "I know you are one, but please be fair."

In recent years, female theologians have been challenging the exclusive masculine references to the deity in the Old and New Testaments. These scholars argue that the male description of God in itself carries the spiritual suggestion that the masculine order of creation is divine. Therefore God must always be referred to as "He." This probing theological inquiry may, in the end, be one of the most provocative contributions of the feminist movement. "God is a Spirit," Jesus told the woman at the well (John 4:24). And to doubting Thomas, in another setting, he reminded, "A spirit hath not flesh and bones . . ." (Luke 24:39) as humans do. So the limitless being of God outstrips our sexual descriptions. God is complete. Our genderizing, with reference to the deity, is a childish way of expressing our own sexual confinement.

The theological question which must be confronted still stands. "Is God an infinite man or is God an infinite spiritual being?" Jesus seemed to support the latter view, even though his radical description of the love of God is stated in fatherly terms. In his discussion with the woman at the well at Sychar, Jesus legitimized the reverent pursuit of an improved description of the nature of God. The question now being raised is whether the masculine "metaphors (in the Bible) do not encourage a double standard for evaluating human beings, in addition to reinforcing an idolatrous description of the deity." The issue is fundamental.

In chapters 1 and 2 of Genesis, Eve is described, in the Hebrew tongue, as *Ezer,* which means "helper." She is an equal partner with Adam. The fact that she was formed from the body of Adam suggests their essential identity and equality. Adam said, "She shall be called Woman because she was taken out of Man." Both Adam and Eve ate the forbidden fruit. And they were both punished with equal severity. God held them equally responsible for the act of disobedience. Thus, it seems unfair to interpret the Genesis account as a female "putdown."

In defense of the woman caught in adultery, Jesus struck a clear blow for equal justice. It was not that he condoned the sin of the woman; but, by his act of intervention, he condemned the double standard which ordered the stoning of the woman and permitted her consort to go free. Whatever he wrote on the ground embarrassed her accusers. Jesus forgave the woman and instructed her to go and sin no more. In the conversation with the Samaritan woman at the well of Sychar, the Master dealt with her questions in a way which gave dignity to the dialogue and the relationship between them. That exchange has left a theological legacy of the highest order, benefitting and challenging all disciples in all the years to come.

Judging from the New Testament description of the relationship between Jesus and women, it appears that he would have surely chosen at least one to share the inner circle of his discipleship; but the culture and customs of ancient Judaism would not have allowed it. It would have added another major impediment and would have provided his enemies with additional ammunition to discredit his mission. And since the secondary place of women was accepted by the women themselves, it would have been even more difficult. In one of his last utterances on the cross, Jesus paid tribute to womanhood by making provision for the care of his mother. Of all of the world's religious leaders and philosophers, no one has even given woman a higher place of honor and respect than Jesus.

At certain points the apostle Paul seemed to insist upon a secondary place for women. In I Corinthians 11:7, he says that the man is "the image and glory of God: but the woman is the glory of the man." Likewise, in his pastoral instruction to young Timothy he says, "Let the woman learn in all silence with all subjection. But I suffer not a woman to teach, nor to usurp authority over the man, but to be in silence. For Adam was first formed, then Eve. And Adam was not deceived, but the woman being deceived was in transgression" (I Timothy 2:8-14).

It is evident here that Paul was reflecting a traditional theological basis for the subjugation of women. This is probably the most forthright statement in the New Testament suggesting a biblical reason for the repression of women. In fact, it is the great apostle's scriptural interpretation, at this point, which justified for centuries traditional church attitudes toward the female sex. Furthermore, Paul's restrictive words to the congregation at Corinth concerning spurious speaking in unknown tongues commands: "Let your women keep silence in the churches: for it is not permitted unto them to speak . . ." (I Corinthians 14:34-35). These are hard words.

But God got hold of Paul in a moment of ecstatic inspiration, and the great apostle penned a message to the congregation at Galatia which supersedes all of his other utterances. It is the message of liberation which speaks the mind of Christ:

> For ye are all the children of God by faith in Christ Jesus. For as many of you as have been baptized into Christ have put on Christ. There is neither Jew nor Greek, there is neither bond nor free, there is neither male nor female: for ye are all one in Christ Jesus. And if ye be Christ's, then are ye Abraham's seed, and heirs according to the promise." (Galatians 3:26-28)

This magnificent statement of the apostle seems to override spiritually his traditional description of the place of women in church and society, as found in other passages. In the new covenant relationship, the confinements of the old are abrogated. Hence, from the lips of

Paul himself comes the liberating word: "Ye are all one in Christ Jesus."

In the First Epistle of Peter there is a restatement of the traditional view, illustrating that Paul's lofty description of the new society in Galatians gradually lost its glow in favor of the reassertion of the ancient interpretation of male domination and female subservience.

In all of human history, up to now, women have always shared disproportionately the world's work load without adequate recognition or reward. This was partially due to traditional attitudes, but there were also survival realities which made the muscular male presence necessary to women. But in recent years Western society has provided survival systems for its constituents which make it possible for men and women to live with a greater degree of independence. Simultaneously, equal opportunity legislation guarantees equal pay for equal work and promotion and position determined by ability, regardless of sex.

But the present trend toward male/female equalization ought not to diminish our appreciation for both the differences and similarities, in form and function, which characterize men and women. There is the story of a man who continually introduced his wife, in the presence of his friends, as his "better half." He seemed to take great pains to insist on this introduction. A bit embarrassed, one of his friends asked him why he made such an emphasis upon his wife being the "better half." The man responded, "So she won't begin to think that she's the whole thing."

This cautious reminder is important to a generation which threatens to turn a remarkable period of male/female social change into a contest between the sexes. Any attempt to assert the priority of one sex over another is destructive. Likewise, any tendency toward a unisexual society, in which men are feminized and woman are masculinized, will result in boredom and sexual confusion. Efforts to normalize homosexuality will pervert the obvious intention of the Creator and escalate the trend toward decadence. God created male and female with marked differences in form and function which complement the unity of society through their mutual male/female interaction and expression.

To celebrate and fortify the marriage relationship does not negate the life of the single person or the childless couple. Human sexuality, which is larger than sexual intimacy, is the expression of a divinely bestowed ingredient which brings balance and vitality to society and, in some sense, to the whole universe as well. Marriage is an intimate covenant relationship between man and woman. In the Western world marriage selection comes through mutual choice. In the East, many marriages are still arranged through mediators, with parental initiation and approval. In the individual selective process, potential partners find each other through association and mutual attraction with the reinforcing incentives of romantic love. In the arranged marriage, on the other hand, the mediator seeks to bring together persons whose potential compatibilities seem self-evident. Romance grows after the ceremonial act of marriage.

But regardless of the procedure which results in the choice of marriage mates, the love relationship develops. Sexual intimacy, working together to achieve common objectives, and sharing a common interpretation of the meaning and purpose of life strengthens commitment. As one author states, "Love does not consist of gazing at each other but in looking outward together in the same direction." Committed marriages are crucial to the health of every society because they provide intimate support relationships between persons, because the creation and nurture of children depend upon the love and stability of parents in a family setting, and because the success or failure of families prophesies the future of a society.

It is God's miraculous gift that within the intimacy of the male/female relationship the conception and birth of children is possible. Without minimizing the importance of other human endeavors, the proper care and nurture of children should be society's first priority. Failure in this endeavor makes all other human accomplishments futile and without purpose. The conception, nurture, and development of human life are the most important tasks on earth.

Christianity's central doctrine is the Incarnation—the assertion that God invested the substance of the divine being in Jesus the Christ. A woman conceived him. Parents nurtured him. Under the careful guidance of Mary and Joseph, the Gospel of Luke says: "And the child . . . waxed strong in spirit, . . . and the grace of God was upon him. . . ." He "increased in wisdom and stature, and in favor with God and man" (Luke 2:40, 52).

During his earthly ministry Jesus gave special importance to the place of children. He put them first on his agenda: "Suffer little children, and forbid them not, to come unto me," he said, "for of such is the kingdom of heaven" (Matthew 19:14). He also had strong words about adult responsibility in connection with the nurture of children and a warning against offenders. "Whoso shall offend one of these little ones which believe in me," said Jesus, "it were better for him(her) that a millstone were hanged about his(her) neck, and that he(she) were drowned in the depth of the sea" (Matthew 18:6).

St. Paul instructed children to obey their parents. But with equal vigor he admonished fathers: "Don't overcorrect your children or make it difficult for them to obey the commandment. Bring them up with Christian teaching in Christian discipline" (Ephesians 6:6; *Phillips*). And to Titus, his son in the gospel, Paul advised: "Teach the young women to love their children" (Titus 2:4).

One child psychologist has underlined the importance of the child-raising enterprise with these words: "You cannot pay anyone to love your child. The monogamous family is the perfect environment for child development, for the incubation of feelings."

Though children are the special responsibility of parents, every male and female in the society shares in the nurturing task. Women and men who have no children after the flesh have equal opportunity and responsibility to involve themselves directly and indirectly in designing a social climate favorable to child development. A society in which adult preferences and adult privileges overshadow the needs and the necessary protections for growing children predicts daily its own demise! Male and female behavior models that "offend" the tender disposition of dependent children can expect the judgment of God! The child-centered society is a healthy society.

At age twenty-eight, after marrying the prime minister of Canada and giving birth to three beautiful children, Margaret Trudeau announced her "abdication." Leaving her husband and children behind, she took off with the following declaration: "I'm going to be working around the world. . . . I'm just being myself. . . . If people want to condemn me as my own person, fine, but don't condemn me as the prime minister's wife, because I abdicate." She made no mention of the children. But can a declaration, a divorce, or an abdication separate any of us from our primary reponsibility?

Somewhere in our forties we reach what one author calls "the deadline decade," when we are preoccupied with a crucial evaluation of where we have been, where we are, and where we are going. Knowing that we have used up more time and energy than we have left, unfulfilled anxiety feelings can reach crisis proportions. But this anxious self-preoccupation gives way when, looking back, we feel the warmth of the new generation we have had a part in shaping. To experience the love and concern of the young as we are growing older is the best of life. To know that those who come after us are adequately prepared in faith, hope, and charity is the only promise on earth that the world can be better in the future than it has been in the past.

If, in the mad rush for self-fulfillment, women and men stumble into selfish isolation, losing the tenderness of mutual graces, demanding more of each other than we are capable of giving, determined to make ourselves happy while abusing the affections of each other, receiving but not giving, we will all be miserable. But if the saving message of the Master has found us, transformed our appetites, and rendered us capable of redemptive living, love will have a place for each of us at the great table where the people of God reach out to feed each other.

Chapter V

Beyond the Law
Galatians 3:24

Jesus began his ministry in a world dominated by Roman law and order. With the striking power of its armies, the genius of its civil administration, and the effectiveness of its legal system, Rome managed the whole of the Western world. The Jews were the subjects of Caesar. Respect for law was fundamental during the days of Rome's ascendancy. But the drain on Rome's resources from continuous wars, the failings of its emperors, and the heavy burdens placed on the shoulders of the poor bred discontent.

Laws are capable of maintaining order when they have the consent and support of the governed. But when laws repress the legitimate expectations of the people, order slowly crumbles. Dr. Martin Luther King, Jr., during the difficult days of the civil rights struggle, taught respect for law. But, with equal vigor, he insisted that unjust laws should be challenged and changed. His commitment to nonviolence, however, led Dr. King to insist that even those who disobeyed unjust laws were bound to pay the penalty for their resistance. In the spirit of Jesus, King's persistent protest continued until bad laws were replaced by good laws.

In the American legal system the Constitution is the basic document. Congressionally enacted laws and judicial decisions are all designed to carry out constitutional purposes. The President, the chief executive of the nation, is sworn to uphold our legal system, serve as the commander-in-chief of the armed forces, and provide leadership necessary to the success of a democratic society.

Ancient Judaism was ruled, religiously, by the Ten Commandments. These were laws given by God and delivered by the hand of Moses. Ancient Israel aspired to be a theocracy, a people governed by God. The first four commandments firmly support the singular sovereignty of God, the King of the universe.

> Thou shalt have no other gods before me.
> Thou shalt not make unto thee any graven image . . .
> Thou shalt not take the name of the Lord thy God in vain . . .
> Remember the sabbath day, to keep it holy.
> (Exodus 20:3-8)

This strong theocentric emphasis in Judaism was meant to be a permanent barrier against any earthly king or emperor who aspired to usurp absolute power. It was a warning against the worship of material objects and a clear call to revere God, and God alone, absolutely. Setting aside a special day of the week for rest and worship was conceived to be a disciplined reminder of the first commitment of the Jewish community to God.

The fifth commandment undergirds the central importance of the family: "Honor thy father and thy mother" (Exodus 20:13). Implicit in this simple admonition is the recogition that respect is the highest expression of love and concern. Family unity requires mutual respect, with deserving parents holding the highest level of responsibility.

The next four commandments are indispensable guidelines to human community life anywhere on earth. It is to be remembered that the Israelites received these laws from Moses when they were wandering in the desert, living in tents. Locks for doors and walls for houses were not a part of their experience. Therefore, to protect the community from the destructiveness of human predators, divine sanction was invoked:

> Thou shalt not kill.
> Thou shalt not commit adultery.
> Thou shalt not steal.
> Thou shalt not bear false witness.
> (Exodus 20:13-16)

No one has a right to take the law into his own hands and kill another person. The marriage covenant is sacred and must be reinforced and protected by the whole community. Stealing and lying are twin destroyers; for, if we cannot trust each other, community life becomes impossible.

The last commandment deals with the psychic aspect of sin: "Thou shalt not covet . . ." (Exodus 20:17). To covet is to cultivate in one's mind unlawful, inordinate, improper, or jealous desires. This commandment recognizes that the contemplation of evil thoughts always precedes evil deeds. So the law admonishes the faithful to protect the inner sanctum of the soul from devious designs lest, in the face of temptation, we sin.

St. Paul described the Mosaic law as a schoolmaster. A more correct translation would be an "attendant, custodian, or guardian." "Schoolmaster" is the Greek word for the servant or slave who was made responsible for the discipline of household children from ages six to sixteen. So, as Paul conceived it, the law was the disciplinarian; but now, through Christ, we are empowered by the Holy Spirit to live above and beyond the demands of the law.

In the Living Bible translation of selected verses from Galatians Paul says:

> Until Christ came we were guarded by the law, kept in protective custody, so to speak, until we could believe in the coming Savior. Let me put it another way. The Jewish laws were our teacher and guide until Christ came to give us right standing with God through faith. But now that Christ has come, we don't need those laws any longer to guard us and lead us to him. For now we are all children of God through faith in Jesus Christ. (3:23-26)

It is as if Paul is remembering the prophetic words of Jeremiah:

> I will put my law in their inward parts, and write it in their hearts; and will be their God, and they shall be my people. And they shall teach no more every man his neighbor, and every man his brother, saying, Know the Lord: for they shall all know me, from the least of them unto the greatest. (Jeremiah 31:33-34)

Under the mandate of the law, Paul is saying, obedience was prompted by necessity and fear; but in Christ we are motivated by the Holy Spirit, which inspires a higher desire to make love the law of life. Certainly Jesus illustrated this truth in his conversation with the rich young ruler. The young man told Jesus he had obeyed all of the commandments of Moses. But Jesus challenged him further, saying: "One thing thou lackest: go thy way, sell whatsoever thou hast, and give to the poor, . . . and come, . . . and follow me" (Mark 10:21). The young man was dismayed when he perceived the requirements of the law of the kingdom of God.

Two little boys were talking about school. The youngest was just learning to spell "cat." The older boy, encountering some difficulty in his school work, said to the younger, "Don't learn to spell 'cat.' If you do, after that the words get harder and harder and harder." So it is with us. Once we understand the meaning of love, everything we say and do becomes more challenging,

Christian theology teaches that salvation is an undeserved gift of God. It is freely given. But the liberty we have received in Christ prepares us for a more excellent self-expression. Salvation is free. Through the cross we are spiritually liberated from both the penalty and the power of sin. But the freedom we have received in Christ anticipates a life lived above and beyond the requirements of the law.

Martin Luther, the great Protestant reformer, received new spiritual illumination when he rediscovered justification by faith through reading Paul's Epistle to the Romans. But he chastized one of his contemporaries, a friend named Johann Agricola, for espousing what Luther called "antinomianism." Agricola was teaching that Christians were no longer obligated to any moral or ethical framework of law. "The Decalog," he declared, "belongs in the courthouse, not in the pulpit. . . . To the gallows with Moses!" Some heretical groups in the early church espoused this view. And there are some nominal Christians today still trying to keep that notion alive. The Epistle of James, originally written as a corrective to the author's understanding of Paul's emphasis on faith, challenged the whole Christian community with the bold declaration: "Faith, if it hath no works, is dead!" (2:17).

In the Sermon on the Mount, Jesus set a standard for his disciples which exceeded by far the expectations of the Mosaic law. The Living Bible translation of this statement in Matthew's Gospel is very explicit.

> Don't misunderstand why I have come—it isn't to cancel the laws of Moses and the warnings of the prophets. No, I came to fulfill them, and make them all come true. With all earnestness I have I say: Every law in the Book will continue until its purpose is achieved. And so if anyone breaks the least commandment, and teaches others to do so, he(she) shall be the least in the Kingdom of Heaven. . . . unless your goodness is greater than that of the Pharisees . . . you can't get into the Kingdom of Heaven at all!" (5:17-20)

The Master's specifics, as recorded in Matthew, are a call to the highest level of practical spirituality. The opening Beatitudes in chapter 5, representing one of the most precious pieces of literary writing on earth, are elaborated upon in the verses and chapters that follow. We are called to be the salt of the earth and the light of the world. We are told that, if we indulge in covetous lusting, we are guilty of the act itself. Divorce is the last option for the disciples of Jesus, with infidelity being the only justifiable cause. When unjustly abused, we are not to strike back, but rather, turn the other cheek as a gesture of reconciliation.

"Love your enemies," the Master commands. "Be ye perfect, even as your Father which is in heaven is perfect" (Matthew 5:48). Give generously and humbly, without thought of reward. Pray quietly and with a sincere heart. Invest your assets in the kingdom of God and remember—you cannot serve two masters. Trust God for everything. Ask, seek, knock, and whatever you need

will be given. Always be on the lookout for false prophets
and remember to build your life on a solid foundation.
These are the rules of the road for the Christian above and
beyond the old requirements of the law of Moses
(Matthew 5–7).

A few months ago on a visit to Scandanavia, I was
talking to a young Swedish pastor. He said that the state
church of Sweden no longer speaks out on moral or
ethical questions. The secular state makes the laws
governing the conduct of the people. Therefore, pastors
feel restricted, almost exclusively, to a supportive
pastoral ministry. The moral and ethical expectations of
Christ are not to be advertised. But what happens to a
society with no absolute frame of reference for its ethics
and morality?

During the revolutionary 1960s, thousands of young
Americans, opposed to the Vietnam War and disillusioned with the American political system, organized
communes, where people could live together, supporting
each other and adopting a more simplified life-style. Love
and concern for each other were to be the cohesion of the
community. But, alas, many of these beautiful experi-
ments fell apart because there was no common commitment to a practical spirituality that expressed itself in
specific definitions of community and mutually accepted
disciplines by which the life of the commune was to be
governed.

Over a decade ago, Rollo May wrote a bestseller
entitled *Love and Will*. At one point he observed:

> The gospel of free expression of every impulse disperses
> experience like a river with no banks, its water spilled and
> wasted as it flows in every direction. The discipline of eros
> (the drive to create and procreate) provides *forms* in

which we can develop and which protect us from
unbearable anxiety. (p. 97)

New phrases are constantly being invented to make old
ideas sound new. One of the contemporary cliches is
"being human." But I have heard few proper definitions
of what is meant by it. If it means the acceptance of some
poorly delineated "I'm O.K., you're O.K." routine, it
cannot be a legitimate part of the Christian life definition.
The life-empowering spiritual medicine which Jesus
offered promised to arouse in us an awareness of the
Divine. At every point, in word and deed, the Master
spread an extraordinary blueprint of excellence before his
followers. The "abundant life" does not suggest the
achievement of the lowest common denominator of our
humanity. Rather, it elicits an appetite for the highest
possible potential . . . the best.

In his parting words to his disciples, Jesus declared:
"He that believeth on me, the works that I do shall
he(she) do also; and greater works than these . . .
because I go unto my Father" (John 14:12). Then he goes
on to add:

> "If you love me, obey me; and I will ask the Father and he
> will give you another comforter, and he will never leave
> you. He is the Holy Spirit, the Spirit who leads into all
> truth. . . . The one who obeys me is the one who loves
> me; and because he loves me, my Father will love
> him(her) also. . . ." (John 14:15-17, 21 *LB*)

So Jesus has promised us the capability and the
empowerment to do the will of God in the world rather
than to follow listlessly the guidance of our own so-called
"humanity." To do the work of Christ in the world is to

imitate the example which he set. Issues of private and public morality must be confronted. Unjust systems and structures which repress and exploit must be removed. Love and justice must walk and work together until the crooked is made straight and the rough places plain.

Chapter VI

Thou Art the Man
II Samuel 12:7-9

Ancient Judaism not only affirmed the existence of one God, but it insisted that God was involved in every detail of the life of the world. This notion of the God who is at work in history gave birth to a peculiar crop of unusual persons called "prophets." The word itself originates from an Akkadian and Arabic rootage. It means "to call" or "to announce." Prophetic utterances were often preceded by the declaratory phrase, "Thus saith the Lord!" So, it may be said, a prophet is one who announces the relevance of God to particular events, personalities, and places. In this sense, the prophet is God's spokesperson.

Hebrew prophets were not certified or approved by any authorizing religious agency. On the contrary, they were considered the direct messengers of God. Their oracles frequently indicted political and religious leaders, pricked the conscience of the people, condemned hypocrisy and sinfulness, and warned the nation against apostasy. Basically, the prophets' message was a call to obedience and repentance. Sometimes they had specific predictions and directions relating to current and future events.

There existed confraternities of ecstatic prophets who associated in charismatic assemblies, spuriously uttering whatever they were inspired to say. But the prophets who are remembered in the Bible seem specifically directed by God to deal with matters relating to the conduct of the nation and the life of the people in particular. Because the prophets were critical and judgmental, they were seldom popular. But the people listened, afraid to repress them, lest they find themselvs opposing God. For all these reasons the life of the prophets was risky. Sometimes they seemed to succeed in their mission. On other occasions they were rebuffed.

Now when David was king of Israel, the book of Samuel records, there was a prophet by the name of Nathan who frequented the king's court (II Samuel 7:1-7). Apparently, David held Nathan in high respect. They consulted when David was considering building the temple. And when the king was on his deathbed, he instructed Nathan and Zadok, the priest, to anoint Solomon as his royal successor. But the event which distinguishes Nathan from all of the other recorded prophets is his encounter with the king over David's infraction of the law and the king's subtle effort to cover up his wrongdoing. The story bears repeating.

One day while David was resting on his roof garden, he saw, in a neighboring court below, a beautiful woman taking a bath. He inquired of his servants as to who she was. He was told that she was Bathsheba, the wife of Uriah the Hittite, an officer in the king's army. Uriah was away fighting the foes of Israel under the command of General Joab. So David sent for Bathsheba. They were intimate. Shortly thereafter, Bathsheba informed the king that she was with child. David was distressed. In order to prevent discovery of his deed, he recalled Uriah

and gave him military leave, hoping Uriah's presence
would shift responsibility for the pregnancy. The king
sent gifts to Uriah's house and bade him to spend some
time at home with Bathsheba. But David's plan went
awry because Uriah, who had been consecrated for
battle, would not violate the taboo. Instead of going
home, as he had been instructed, he humbly went to the
servants' quarters in the palace and remained there,
awaiting orders from the king.

When David discovered that his plan had aborted, he
called Uriah to his court and gave him a message to
deliver to General Joab. Uriah was not aware that the
letter instructed Joab to place him in the thick of the
battle so he would be slain. When General Joab received
the king's order, he gave Uriah command over a cluster of
soldiers and sent them into the most dangerous battle
zone. As Uriah and his soldiers moved into the fray, they
ran headlong into the fury of the opposition. So Uriah and
most of his battalion were slain. And when David
received the word that Uriah was dead, he took
Bathsheba for his own wife.

Suspicions arose concerning the coincidence of Uriah's
death and the king's marriage. Words of accusation were
whispered in low tones within and without the king's
court. Gossipers, not knowing all the facts, added
extenuating details, while the king's defenders used their
influence to repress the truth. There was no one in all of
Israel who would speak an open word against the king.
Some tried to excuse the king's action by pointing out that
Uriah was a Hittite, a member of another race. So they
dismissed the seriousness of the act by demeaning the
personhood of Uriah. After all, he was only a foreigner.
But the sensitive souls in Israel realized that the king's

action against Uriah endangered the civil rights of every citizen in the land.

One day when the king's court agenda was unhurried, Nathan was ushered into the king's presence to share a concern. He began with a story about a poor man who had one ewe lamb and a rich man who had a great herd of cattle. But when a traveler came to visit the rich man, instead of using one of his own herd, he seized the poor man's lamb and slew it for the feast. Now when David heard the story, he stood upright, incensed. "Where is that unjust man?" he exclaimed. "He will pay for his deed." Then Nathan, the prophet, slowly raising his trembling arm, pointed his finger at the king and exclaimed, "Thou art the man!" (II Samuel 12:7).

In the whole history of the Hebrew prophets, this was the most traumatic moment of them all, a prophet's accusing Israel's greatest king of breaking the law and attempting to cover up his crime. Surprised and stunned, David slumped back in his chair, in the presence of his courtiers, and exclaimed: "I have sinned . . ." (12:13).

Nathan's courageous confrontation was the most important happening in Israel that day. He aligned himself with all of the prophets of God, in every age, who place their earthly lives and fortunes in jeopardy rather than remain silent when the truth has no spokesperson. Some scholars who have studied the ancient manuscripts doubt that Nathan, who appeared to have such a special relationship with King David, would have jeopardized their friendship by confronting the king in court. But the Nathan story is another indication of biblical credibility. The Bible tells the truth even though it may embarrass its greatest heroes. David was guilty of a very common sin

upon earth, the abuse of power. And Nathan risked his
life to speak for God.

Every person, rich and poor, has power of some sort
and in some degree. Each person, consciously or
unconsciously, exercises that power to influence other
persons and situations according to certain preferences.
The outcome of any event or the expression of any person
may be altered according to the way power is applied. If
power is employed selfishly, without reference to moral
or ethical absolutes, people get hurt. When power is used
responsibly, governed by the love ethic, people are
helped. Ruthless and violent uses of power are often
couched in seemingly harmless legalistic language. At
other times, abusive power is masked by cloaks of
compassion, justified by popular prejudice, or employed
under the pretense of rendering some assistance. But the
David/Uriah story has all of the familiar markings of
contemporary power encounters.

When power pyramids into giant international corporations, immense political patronage systems, mam-
moth military machines, monolithic religious institutions;
or when it finds its way into the singular grasp of dictators
or kings, moral and ethical controls are more difficult.
That is why the role and credibility of the communications
media is so vital. Someone must be continually digging
into the public and private life of persons, corporations,
and institutions, which exercise such pervasive influence
over the lives of so many people. Wrongdoing must be
continually discovered and exposed.

Dr. Karl Menninger's pertinent question, "Whatever
became of sin?" is relevant. Psychotherapists, sociolo-
gists, and even theologians were disturbed by Menninger's revival of the "sin" vocabulary, for sin is no
longer a serious consideration for modern sophisticates.

Dr. Menninger defined sin as "behavior that violates the moral code or the individual conscience or both; behavior which pains or harms or destroys my neighbor—or me, myself." If a society no longer gives credence to moral or ethical absolutes, derived from historical experience and biblical testimony, it is more difficult to appeal to conscience.

Whether our conception of sin is biblical, situational, psychological, or sociological, the content of Menninger's definition deserves a hearing. Sin implies there is a standard recognized by the society and enforced with society's support. David's act of repentance was prompted by the fact that the Mosaic Law permeated the life of Israel. Therefore, in the face of Nathan's revelation, even the king had to recant. For he had not only violated the person of Uriah, but David had also offended God!

A few years ago the National Science Foundation sponsored a research project involving twenty-four sixth-grade classes in seventeen different California schools. The students were tested on their attitude toward cheating. The test was on some objective subject matter, and the students were promised prizes for excellence. During the course of the examination there were opportunities for students to cheat. Of course, they were unaware that the temptation had been prearranged. The study discovered that those who resisted the chance to cheat, because they believed it was wrong, became stronger in their opposition of cheating. But the students who cheated became more lenient in their attitudes towards cheating and more defensive with reference to cheaters. When a society becomes morally indecisive, its character and commitment erodes.

In the fourteenth century, a Czechoslovakian priest by

the name of John Huss raised his voice against the power abuses of the religious hierarchy of the medieval church. In addition to his call for freedom of the pulpit, Huss demanded that the sacrament, both bread and wine, be served to the laity. But the thing that angered the religious and political establishment most was his insistence that the priests and the hierarchy give up their vast land holdings and their luxurious living and conform to their vows of poverty, chastity, and obedience. Huss incured even greater wrath when he demanded that public and private sins be punished regardless of the prominence or position of the persons involved. His was a cry for equal justice under the law. He raised the rules of Jesus to a high level in his preaching and referred to the Sermon on the Mount as the Magna Carta of the Kingdom of God. For his prophetic bravery, Huss was burned at the stake on July 6, 1415. A century later, Martin Luther nailed his ninety-five theses to the door of the cathedral at Wittenberg, sparking the great sixteenth-century reformation. Speaking to a group of his supporters, Luther declared, "We are all the Hussites." Even today, behind the Iron Curtain, the presidential flag of Czechoslovakia bears the inscription of John Huss, "Truth will prevail."

Twenty years ago, C. Wright Mills wrote an article in *Nation* magazine entitled, "A Pagan Sermon to the Christian Clergy." His hard jibes are worth repeating.

> Religion today . . . does not originate; it reacts. It does not denounce; it adapts. It does not set forth new models of conduct and sensibility; it imitates. Its rhetoric is without deep appeal; the worship it organizes is without piety. . . . Christianity is part of the moral defeat of men today. Perhaps it is no longer important enough to be considered a cause.

Dr. Mills' despair regarding the church is matched by a word of caution coming from Dr. Hans Küng, the prominent Tübingen Roman Catholic theologian. He says, "A church can lose its soul by being so progressive that it fails to remain what it is in all the change *or* by being so conservative in remaining unchanged that it does not become anew what it ought to be." This observation increases the importance of keeping Christ central in the continuing effort of the church to be faithful to its discipleship. Whether the church should continue old traditions and standards or adopt new practices should not depend upon opinion polls or the judgment of researchers and scholars. Scholars disagree with each other. Our model of measurement must be the message of Jesus Christ as revealed in the Gospels and interpreted in the Epistles.

Dr. James Cone struck a hard blow when he said in *A Black Theology of Liberation* that

> There can be no Christian theology which is not identified unreservedly with those who are humiliated and abused. . . . It is impossible to speak of the God of Israelite history, who is the God who revealed himself in Jesus Christ, without recognizing that he is the God of those who labor and are heavy laden. (pp. 17-18).

The current interest in personal religion must not ignore the issues of international justice, public ethics and morality, racism, and sex discrimination. We are called upon to meddle, to investigate, to inquire, to speak out, and to sacrifice our personal security when sacrifice is required in order to speak the truth and do the truth in season and out of season.

The life of Jesus, the Incarnate One, is the model that God has given us to follow. Early in his ministry the

Master announced his purposes in the synagogue of Nazareth by reading from the prophet Isaiah:

"The Spirit of the Lord is upon me, because he hath anointed me to preach the gospel to the poor; he hath sent me to heal the brokenhearted, to preach deliverance to the captives, and recovering of sight to the blind, to set at liberty them that are bruised, to preach the acceptable year of the Lord" (Luke 4:18-19).

The Gospels detail how Jesus lived out this prophetic intentionality. He proclaimed the Kingdom of God, healed the sick and raised the dead, befriended little children, released the woman about to be stoned, talked theology at the well of Sychar, shook his finger in the face of the hypocritical Pharisees, and took a twisted rope and drove the moneychangers out of the temple.

It was the prophetic aspect of the ministry of Jesus that incurred the wrath of the power brokers of his day. They crucified him. But this effort to kill the Truth released the great resource of God's redemptive power. God translated the ignominy of the cross into a resurrection victory and raised up a host of disciples and prophets to carry the Good News

to the uttermost part of the earth.

Chapter VII

There Is a Path
Job 28:7

Job is the story of a man struggling with the problem of human suffering. According to the teaching of the ancient Jews, Job understood that divine judgment and suffering were a consequence of sin. But the thing that perplexed him was the suffering of the righteous. Job himself was the subject of his own distress, for he had been stripped of all of his possessions and had lost his children and his servants. Bereft of health and friends, he languished on an ash heap, accompanied only by his grieving wife. When Job's friends heard of his misfortune, they came to commiserate. When they arrived, they were appalled at the degradation of their once prosperous companion. They, too, according to the teaching of Judaism, were convinced that all suffering resulted from sin. Hence, much of their early conversation was spent in trying to assist Job in remembering the misdeeds which had contributed to his downfall. Though they had confidence in Job's integrity, they were convinced that he had some hidden fault. But Job insisted upon his innocence, even though his strong self-vindication put his faith in God to the test.

In the prologue to the Job story, a contest between God

and the Devil is described as the cause of Job's travail. But in the narrative itself, Job seems completely unaware of this motif. In fact, some scholars believe the present prologue to the book of Job was a latter addition.

From the very outset, Job is confounded by his situation and seems to have no adequate explanation. Near the end of the narrative, Job is declared guilty of a singular, monumental sin: pride. The fact that he considered himself undeserving of suffering suggested an exaggerated opinion of his own righteousness. Secondly, Job's guilt is intensified by the arrogance of attempting to match his finite wits against the infinite capacities of God. He is declared guilty of demanding answers which, if given, he would not be able to comprehend because of his human restrictions. Finally, God crashes in on Job with massive, overpowering questions which challenge the arrogance of Job and incriminate the credibility of his inquiries.

So Job is left with the problem of undeserved suffering and unanswered questions. His guilt, common to all sensitive human questioning, is simply asking "Why?" In the end Job decides that faith in God, even without all the answers, is better than life without faith and without God. So he is persuaded to respond to the Deity thus:

> I know that you are all-powerful: what you conceive, you can perform. I am the man who obscured your designs with my empty-headed words. I have been holding forth on matters I cannot understand, on marvels beyond me and my knowledge. . . . But now, having seen you with my own eyes, I retract all I have said, and in dust and ashes I repent" (Job 42:1-6; *JB*).

Chapter 28 of Job's discourse was a favorite biblical passage of one of my college classmates. It begins with a rehearsal of some of the remarkable exploits of human technology. Human ingenuity has dug deeply into the recesses of the earth, discovering and exploiting its resources. Then verse 7 introduces the notion that "there is a path" beyond everything that human genius has yet unveiled. This, indeed, is a fascinating way for the author to lead us into a deeper discussion of the inner range of the secrets of the universe, beyond material findings. Obviously, the path he is referring to is the way to God.

There follows a brief, but exciting, portrayal of the handiwork of God in nature, climaxed with the piercing question: "Where shall wisdom be found?" In response, nature cries out that the answer cannot be found in the depths of her riches. So the inquirer raises, with even stronger voice, the question: "Whence then cometh wisdom? and Where is the place of understanding?" Death, the imponderable, denies that it holds the clue. So God, alone, must be turned to for the answer. The divine response is finally rendered in the last verse of the chapter: "The fear of the Lord, that is wisdom; and to depart from evil is understanding."

Beyond all of the other considerations in the book of Job, the content of this twenty-eighth chapter deserves thoughtful attention. There is a path to God, the author is saying. Finding God is finding wisdom. And wisdom is reverence for God and resisting evil. Reverence is an attitude toward God and God's created universe which bespeaks respect, appreciation, and singular adoration. Righteousness suggests a sense of responsibility for the state of human affairs in the world in response to the wisdom and guidance of God.

That portion of God's created universe which is controlled by human choice depends upon human faithfulness. Evil, by whatever explanation or origin, is

the abuse of our God-given freedom of choice. Therefore, in the struggle against evil, justice and love must be
invested in every human circumstance. Personal, social,
economic, and political issues, therefore, hold a prominent place in the portfolio of the righteous. That is
wisdom!

There are at least three levels of learning. The first is
the acquisition of knowledge. Where there is no
knowledge there is ignorance, and ignorance is the enemy
of truth. Knowledge is enlightenment, the foundation of
wisdom. The second level of learning is understanding. It
is knowing how one bit of knowledge relates to another
bit of knowledge. Discovering relationships between
seemingly unrelated bits of knowledge is the highest
order of understanding. The third level of learning is
wisdom, perceiving the immediate and ultimate meaning
of what is known and understood.

The methodology of science is adequate for levels one
and two; but the third level, wisdom, requires the
involvement of other disciplines: psychology, philosophy: and religion. Wisdom takes a step beyond the
empirical findings of the scientist and enters the realm of
intellectual speculation and conjecture. Beyond the
practical concerns of survival, wisdom deals with the
introspective questions: "Who am I?" "Why am I here?"
"What is my destiny?" These serious concerns have given
rise to a thoughtful community of seekers and of
speculative thinkers whose disciplined investigations and
research probe such matters as life and death, health and
suffering, righteousness and evil, joy and sorrow. Science
asks the basic question, "How?" Philosophy and religion
push the inquiry one step further and ask, "Why?"

The world is filled with ideas aimed at helping human
beings to find and travel that "path" referred to in the

book of Job. Buddhism, for example, which influences Asia's millions, teaches that life is misery and decay. There is no ultimate reality, visible or invisible. Desire, the accumulated aggressions which grow out of human questing, is, according to Buddhism, the basic human problem. Desire makes persons the slavish servants of the unreal self. Salvation comes through right deeds and meditation which finally enable the achievement of a state of being called nirvana, union with the void . . . a state of nothingness.

Islam, the dominant religion of the Arab world, means submission to God, who is merciful and just. Human beings, according to the teachings of Islam, on the other hand, are limited, sinful, and constantly led astray by Satan. The Devil is interpreted to be a disobedient angel of God. Allah gave Muhammad the Koran to instruct his followers in the proper path. Repentance and submission by the faithful will finally obtain a heavenly reward. But the sinful and unbelieving will be damned in Hell, the Koran teaches.

Hinduism, having its greatest arena of influence in India, asserts that there is one divine principle in the universe. The manifestation of the many Gods prevalent in Hinduism all reflect this central unifying principle. Human beings are related to that principle though they seem to be separate creatures, samsara, the continuous process of birth, death, and rebirth, provides an opportunity for the elevation of persons in their next reincarnation or the lowering of their status or caste, according to their conduct in the previous life. The past deeds of the individual are called karma. Escape from the tyranny of one's karma and the endless anxieties of samsara is achieved only by self-purification and devotion.

Disillusioned with the effect of organized religion on the life of Europe's majority, Karl Marx completely repudiated the religious attempt to provide a path for human fulfillment. In a complete turnabout he offered the radical preference of a life philosophy which concerns itself only with that which is tangible and visible. According to Marx, the economic situation is the key to human degradation or human salvation. The development of a classless society, he predicted, would provide the ultimate solution to human problems and render prevailing religious interpretations unnecessary and obsolete. In his repudiation of religion, Marx admitted violent revolution was the only recourse in overcoming the odds of power vested in the upper-class control system over the destiny of the impoverished majorities of the world.

In the arena of individual pathfinding, psychotherapy has more and more replaced traditional religious interpretations. For example, there is the analytical approach to personality, which proposes to free individuals from conflict between their innate desires and the expectations of their social situation by helping them to become aware of the problem of conflict and to find release from it. The assumption of psychotherapy is that once the individual perceives the nature of his or her difficulty, such self-understanding will also reveal the path to deliverance. Second, there has been a major emphasis on the purely behavioral aspects of the life of persons. This discipline begins with an analysis of negative environmental conditions which provoke undesirable behavior in persons. Through studies of bodily processes and with the use of control techniques of various kinds, including the careful administration of drugs, new life is promised through biological manipulation. Humanists, on the other hand, argue that self-actualization is the primary human need. For them, life enrichment and fulfillment are stressed rather than the curative techniques. Salvation comes when one's own emotional experiences are the sole focus of the whole personality.

Recently, a growing emphasis has developed in what is called the "transpersonal" path. Here, the individual is led to find mastery over life situations through directing consciousness toward union with the universe. Training of the will, the discipline of special diet and exercises, and transcendental meditation are prescribed to give assurance of success in this quasi-mystical approach to self-realization.

A review of some of the many paths illustrates that the restless search for the one path which will provide the answer to the age-old questions of identity and destiny has not ceased. In fact, modern human beings, more than any of their predecessors, are committing a great deal of time and money in pursuit of the ultimate way.

One day a disciple of Jesus named Thomas had an interesting conversation with the Master. Jesus had just shared with his disciples the fact that he would soon leave them, but he was going to prepare a place for them and, eventually, would return for them. Then he said: "Whether I go ye know, and the way ye know." It was then that Thomas intervened, saying in effect: "No, we don't. We haven't any idea where you are going, so how can we know the way?" The Master's answer has become a one-line Christian classic: "I am the way, the truth, and the life." (John 14:1-6). Reviewing that conversation calls to mind Job's interesting affirmation, "There is a path," and Job's pertinent question, "Where can wisdom be found?" Jesus spoke to these concerns almost two

thousand years ago. No honest seeker is faithful to the
"search" unless he or she takes a careful look at the basic
teaching revealed in the words and deeds of the Master.

First of all, the Master taught the existence of one God.
He personalized his interpretation of the nature of God
by describing the Deity in the likeness of a loving father.
His parable of the lost sheep and the story of the prodigal
son gave the multitudes who listened, and the generations
since, a refreshingly warm feeling for the intimate interest
of the transcendent God in the detailed experiences of
persons. He translated Judaism's "King of the Universe"
into the language of love.

After Jesus' temptation experience in the mountain,
Mark records that Jesus came among the people
proclaiming that the "kingdom of God is at hand" (Mark
1:15). It was a message of the immediacy of God's
program of personal and social transformation. Much of
the excitement which followed the original utterances of
Jesus resulted from the rising expectations of his hearers.
They could share a place in God's kingdom right now.
The compensations of religious faith did not need to wait
until the life after death. When the Master's critics
taunted him, saying, "When will the kingdom of God
begin?" Jesus replied: "The kingdom of God isn't
ushered in with visible signs. You won't be able to say, 'It
has begun here in this place or there in that part of the
country.' For the kingdom of God is within you" (Luke
17:20-21 *LB*). Jesus taught that God is in residence in
persons right now. The transformation and renewal of
individuals is the beginning and the extension of the
kingdom of God. What an exciting idea!

When Jesus stood trial before Pontius Pilate for
preaching the coming of his kingdom, the Roman
governor inquired, "Are you the King of the Jews?" Jesus

responded, "I am not an earthly king. If I were, my
followers would have fought when I was arrested. . . .
But my kingdom is not of this world" (John 18:33-36 *LB*).
Earthly kingdoms are established in violence, with the
sword. But the kingdom of God comes through the
redemptive influence of love.

Jesus disassociated the coming of his kingdom from the
revolutionary history of previous volatile prophets who
had fought to liberate their nations with the sword. So the
Master completed his threefold description of the *Now*
kingdom. It indwells all who gain citizenship through the
transforming power of the love of God in Jesus Christ; it is
a kingdom whose ultimate triumph is already assured and
whose final actualization is yet to be.

In his famous discourse, recorded in John's Gospel,
Jesus said, "I am come that they might have life, and that
they might have it more abundantly" (John 10:10). The
slovenly and indifferent are suddenly given new incen-
tive. Every person may now anticipate the highest level of
self-development and fulfillment. Boredom with routine
and the wastefulness of losing life-styles are swept away.
Fresh enthusiasm is provided. It is now possible for each
person to become what God intended him or her to be.

One night Nicodemus, a prominent Pharisee, came
privately to inquire into the Master's doctrines. "We
know that God is with you," he said. "Otherwise, you
would not be able to do the miracles we have seen. But
how can ordinary people ever experience a life filled with
the spiritual empowerment you possess?" Jesus answered: "Except a man be born again. . . . That which is
born of flesh is flesh; and that which is born of Spirit is
spirit" (John 3:3). Jesus made it clear that each person
needs to experience his or her own personal "moment of
truth," a time when human excuses and defenses give way

to an humble, honest, openness to the presence and the power of the Holy Spirit of God. The acknowledgment of sin and insufficiency, the recognition of the saving grace of God revealed in Jesus Christ, and the willingness to receive the gift of God's salvation bring electrifying consequences and new life.

One day when Jesus was alone with his disciples, he placed before them the ultimate demand:

> Anyone who wants to follow me must put aside his(her) own desires and conveniences and carry his(her) cross with him(her) every day and keep close to me. Whoever loses his(her) life for my sake will save it, but whoever insists on keeping his(her) life will lose it." (Luke 9:23-24 *LB*)

Other prophets and philosophers had sought to promote their appeal to persons by catering to their ego and personal ambitions, but Jesus made personal sacrifice central to his discipleship recipe. In essence he said that true happiness is found in a life that is committed, unselfish, and sacrificial. The cross, however, is not interpreted by Jesus as a burdensome joy-killer. On the contrary, it is the clue to self-realization. But the selfish life-style, Jesus predicts, will always end in disappointment.

When he broke the bread and shared the cup with his disciples in the Upper Room on the eve before his crucifixion, Jesus said, "This is my body which is given for you. . . . This is my blood, which is shed for you. . . ." Here the incarnate revelation of God in Jesus Christ interpreted the highest order of suffering, the vicarious giving of one's self in order to redeem the lives of others.

On the first day of the week, when the angel of the Lord rolled the stone away and the resurrected Christ stepped out into history victorious, Christian hope was born. The path through the valley of the shadow of death was transformed from a fearful cavern into an eternal corridor.

The abundant life, so vividly describd by Jesus, was given an everlasting dimension. Quoting the prophet Isaiah, St. Paul exclaimed, "Death is swallowed up in victory."

Along the Christian path, desire is sanctified and redirected. It is not repressed; it is reborn. Desire is not condemned; it is glorified. All our human endowments are lifted to a new level of expression. Selfhood, sexuality, social relationships are dignified. The Christian pilgrim can walk and not be weary, run and not faint. For the strengthening companion for the journey is the Lord of Hosts. "Therefore," says St. Paul, "be ye steadfast, unmoveable, always abounding in the work of the Lord, forasmuch as ye know that your labor is not in vain in the Lord" (I Corinthians 15:58).

We have found the proper path to reverence, and we have discovered the trail of righteousness . . . by faith! "Thanks be to God who giveth us the victory through our Lord Jesus Christ."

Chapter VIII

Divine Surprises
John 1-2

Now and then we are surprised to meet a person of outstanding merit whose point of origin gives no hint of greatness. Little Falls, Minnesota, for example, was a town of no reputation. But it was here where America's most famous aviator spent much of his childhood. Charles A. Lindberg, the troubled hero, had unpromising beginnings. Bethlehem, in far off Judea, was not famous at the time Samuel paid a visit to Jesse, eight centuries before the coming of Christ. Samuel was the chief judge in Israel, a man who had found favor with God and the people. He had been instructed by Jehovah to anoint a new king. In Bethlehem, Samuel found and anointed a young man named David. And David became Israel's greatest monarch. Those who knew Montgomery, Alabama, best would have thought it to be the last place on earth to give birth to a black civil rights movement in America. But in 1956, Montgomery, the "Cradle of the Confederacy," introduced to the world America's most dynamic advocate of social change, Dr. Martin Luther King, Jr.

God has a way of introducing surprises in the most unlikely places and through the life and work of unexpected people. There is an old Hebrew proverb of timeless wisdom which reads:

> Underestimate no man
> Revile no thing;
> For everything has its place,
> And every man his hour.

Frequently, the Bible begins an account with the words "in the fulness of time." So, it appears, when God is ready to speak or act, the place and the person through whom the message comes are beyond the authority or control of human selection. For this reason, the account of the beginning of the ministry of Jesus underlines an object lesson from the Word of God. According to John's Gospel, after John the Baptist had baptized Jesus, two of John's disciples deserted him and began to follow the Master. They spent a day listening to Jesus. Then Andrew, one of the two, was so impressed by what he heard that he went out to find his brother Simon. When he had located Simon, laying hold upon him, he exclaimed, "We have found the Messiah," and he led his brother to Jesus.

Now Andrew's messianic description of Jesus had sensational connotations. This title aroused deeply emotional religious responses among the Jews. The word "Messiah" means "the anointed one." In Judaism it is related to the ancient theocratic ideal. The true leader or king is one who is chosen, anointed by God. Jesus entered Jewish history at a time when the nation had gone through a series of frustrating defeats. Israel yearned for deliverance. The messianic hope in the first century had an interesting combination of ingredients. There was, on the one hand, the supernatural expectation of the coming of the "Son of man." This quasi–angelic leader was expected to bring to pass the culminating act of judgment against all of Israel's oppressors and restore to the chosen people their rightful place in the plan of God. But there was also an earthly expectation, dating from the recollection of Israel's "Golden Age," when David was the king. So there was connected with Hebrew messianism the notion of the coming of a king like David who would lead the nation to power and prominence again. Andrew's message to Simon Peter, therefore, combined these most earnest expectations. The Messiah personifies fulfillment of the divine promise. He moves and changes the course of history according to God's plan.

After Andrew and Peter had joined the ranks of Jesus, Philip responded to the call. He, too, was greatly impressed. Filled with enthusiasm, he sought out his friend Nathaniel, saying, "We have found him, of whom Moses . . . and the prophets, did write." It was then that Nathaniel raised the crucial question, "Can there any good thing come out of Nazareth?" And Philip responded: "Come and see." Nathaniel was a native of Cana of Galilee, the place where Jesus had attended the wedding feast. Cana was only a few miles from Nazareth. Perhaps it was the long-standing rivalry between the two towns which prompted Nathaniel's initial resistance. But, finally, Nathaniel did come to Jesus. After meeting the Master and talking to him, he declared: "Rabbi, thou art the Son of God; thou art the King of Israel."

But Jesus continued to have rejection problems. After he read from the book of Isaiah in the synagogue of Nazareth, his home town, some members of the congregation took offense. In anger they forced him to leave the city and threatened to kill him, but he escaped. Furthermore, Matthew records another disppointment in

Jesus' home town. The people were astonished at his teaching, but some of them vigorously disagreed with some of the things that he said. So, the opposition exclaimed:

Is not this the carpenter's son? is not his mother called Mary? and his brethren, James, and Joses, and Simon, and Judas? And his sisters, are they not all with us? Whence then hath this man all these things? and they were offended in him. But Jesus said unto them, a prophet is not without honor, save in his own country, and in his own house. And he did not many mighty works there because of their unbelief. (Matthew 13:55-58)

Each of the Synoptic Gospels records that the chief priests and scribes questioned the authority of the Master. Unwilling to accept the content of his teaching, they attempted to discredit him by raising questions about his credentials. He had not been approved or certified. He had not taken proper instruction from the religious establishment.

But what did Jesus say and do that was considered so offensive? Why did the religious leaders want to get rid of him? First of all, he came from the ranks of the poor. Hence, he had no support base among the power brokers of Israel. Joseph, his earthly father, was a carpenter. Jesus, after the custom of his time, was doubtless trained in the same vocation. So the Master's tastes, his vocabulary, his illustrations, and his primary interests were rooted in the concerns of the poor. Dr. Howard Thurman, in his *Jesus and the Disinherited,* argues that one of the reasons affluent Christians have difficulty with the gospel is because its application has been distorted. It must always be rememberd, says Dr. Thurman, that Jesus was a Jew, a member of a despised race. He was a poor man's son who worked with his hands, and he was a member of a nation under the control and dominion of imperialistic Rome.

> Christianity, . . . in the mind of (Jesus) . . . appears as a technique of survival for the oppressed. That it became, through the intervening years, a religion of the powerful and the dominant, used sometimes as an instrument of oppression must not tempt us into believing that it was thus in the mind and life of Jesus. [p. 29]

It is understandable, therefore, why Mark records that the "common people heard him gladly" (Mark 12:37). His disciples were ordinary men, without fame titles, or prestigious pedigree.

At first, it appeared, Jesus restricted his message to the Jews. But later he seemed to direct his gospel to anyone who would receive the message. He challenged the racism of the Jews by making the despised Samaritans the heroes of his stories. It was insult enough when the priest and the Levite in the Jericho road story were made to appear as hypocrites, but to make the Samaritan, who helped the man who had been beaten and robbed, the hero was unforgivable. The Samaritans were a racially mixed people. They were Jews who had intermarried with Assyrian settlers centuries before. Their religion was Hebraic combined with pagan influences. The Jews considered them inferior and insisted upon separateness. So, when Jesus made the priest and the Levite the culprits of his story and pictured the Samaritan as the one who displayed care and concern, his Jewish hearers were incensed.

His conversation with the Samaritan woman at the well of Sychar is a theological gem. It opened the door of religious inquiry and exploded provincial conceptions of the nature of God. The fact that Jesus insisted upon traveling through Samaria and talking freely with the people violated an age-old Jewish taboo.

Perhaps the most startling thing Jesus did was to shift the emphasis of religion from ritual and doctrine to the concerns of people. Hebrew religious legalism tended to make the letter of the law central while neglecting the spirit of personal compassion with reference to those who had broken the law. When Jesus was criticized for permitting his disciples to pluck corn on the sabbath, he said, "The sabbath was made for man, and not man for the sabbath" (Mark 2:27). Over the protests of the scribes and the Pharisees, he healed the man with the withered hand on the sabbath day, leaving his critics with the question; "Is it lawful on the sabbath days to do good?" (Luke 6:9). Jesus did not intend to dismiss the importance of the sabbath. After all, it was prescribed by the Torah. But he wanted the people, especially the Pharisees, to understand that the God of the sabbath was the God of compassion whose first interest was in the welfare of the people.

Two charges were leveled against Jesus by his enemies after he had chased the moneychangers out of the temple. Before the Sanhedrin, the religious court of the Jews, he was accused of calling himself the Son of God. But when they brought him before Pontius Pilate, the charge was treason. Jesus preached the coming of the kingdom of God, which seemed to some inimical to the best interests of Rome; so he was suspected of subversion.

But the two charges which contributed to his conviction confirm for all succeeding generations the most remembered truths concerning Jesus of Nazareth. His sonship suggested his identity with God; so the doctrine of the Incarnation was formulated to express the uniqueness of his person and witness. His kingship is remembered with both reflection and anticipation.

At the first ecumenical council of the church, convened in Nicaea by the Emperor Constantine in A.D. 325, a creedal statement was authorized, describing the nature of Christ. The Greek word *Homoousion,* which means "of one and the same nature" with God, was used to express the unity of Christ with God. So the Incarnation, stemming from the Master's own declaration and the conviction of his followers, became the standard doctrinal interpretation of his person. His kingship is attested to by the church's understanding of the kingdom of God as both a present fact in the life of the believer and an eschatological anticipation yet to be fulfilled. But theologizing about Jesus should never be a substitute for the application of his well-defined and demonstrated teachings in resolving the issues of sin and injustice in the world.

In the history of the whole human race, Jesus is God's greatest single revelation. To reflect upon his life, teachings, deeds, death, and resurrection is to perceive the day-by-day relevance of his Word to all of the common issues which we continually confront. One modern creedal statement, attempting to set forth with greater clarity the glory which we beheld in him describes him as:

> Son of God and Son of man,
> The gift of the Father's unfailing grace,
> The ground of our hope,
> And the promise of our deliverance
> From sin and death.

Chapter IX

Now I See
John 9:25

All the recorded acts and sayings of Jesus could be crammed into a few typewritten pages. But, amazingly, these vignettes of the Master's words and works have provoked more books and speeches than the life of any person who has ever lived. To read an account of an act in the life of Jesus is to view an event which grows in meaning the more it is reread. This is certainly the case with the story of the blind man who received his sight on the sabbath. The thing that got it all started was a question from one of the disciples: "Master, why was this man born blind?" (John 9:2; *LB*). The disciples seemed more concerned about the theology surrounding the blind man's situation than the condition of the blind man himself. Jewish religious tradition taught that birth defects resulted from inherited sin. But Jesus apparently rejected this teaching. Instead he said this was an opportunity "to demonstrate the power of God" (9:3).

Then Jesus took spittle, mixed it with dirt, made a small mud pack and smeared a little over each of the blind man's eyes. He said to the man, "Go and wash in the Pool of Siloam" (9:6). The man did what he was told. Suddenly, he could see. When his friends inquired, he told them what had happened. But the critical Pharisees, who were listening in, quickly concluded that even if a miracle had occurred, it was the work of an evil agent; for no God-fearing person in Israel would make a mud pack on the sabbath day. So the Pharisees said to the man who had been healed, "Give glory to God, not to Jesus, for we know Jesus is an evil person." It was then that the beleaguered former blind man exclaimed, "I don't know whether he is good or bad, but I know this: *I was blind, and now I see!* (9:25). Later Jesus returned and the man confessed his faith and became one of the Master's followers.

Personal experience has always been the doorway through which individuals have found faith. Children, born and nurtured by Christian parents and raised in Christian homes, may never remember a time of unbelief. But there are millions of unbelievers who have found faith because they have experienced the healing power of God. One fact is clear—the Gospels testify throughout to the healing power of Jesus. Likewise, in the apostolic church, healing was an integral part of the Christian ministry. But contemporary mainline Christianity tends to leave the healing ministry to sect groups and self-appointed independent preachers. Having constructed great cathedrals, accumulated assets and investments, and increased in membership, institutional Christianity displays its power and glory in material possessions. No longer can the church say, like Peter and John at the Beautiful Gate, "Silver and gold have I none . . ."; but neither can the church say, "Take up thy bed and walk."

John Wesley, the father of Methodism, once said:

I am not afraid that the people called Methodists should ever cease to exist, either in Europe or America. But I am

afraid, lest they should exist only as a dead sect, having
the form of religion without power. And this undoubtedly
will be the case unless they hold fast to the doctrine, spirit,
and discipline with which they first set out.

In recent years we have seen the emergence of what has
been called, "the charismatic movement," with its
emphasis on the work of the Holy Spirit. Unfortunately,
some of its proponents have placed their primary
emphasis on tongue-speaking, a legitimate spiritual
expression, but always a source of controversy in the
church. Generally, charismatics have blessed the church
with a new awareness of divine gifts and divine power.
Wherever polarization and conflict have taken place, it is
because charismatics and their opponents have both been
unfaithful to the directives and disciplines of scripture.

The emphasis upon the applied power of the Holy
Spirit is not the introduction of a new doctrine. It has
always been central in the history of the church. The Holy
Spirit is not the recognition of a new religious ingredient.
Rather, it simply calls to mind that the God of creation,
the One who recreates and sustains, is still at work in the
world. Therefore, all human needs and all human
situations may share in the supplementing strength of
God at all times and in all things.

A story is told of a woman whose washing machine
broke down. She tampered with it for a while, then wrote
a note to her supplier, detailing the nature of the ailment
and suggesting what she thought needed to be done. But
days passed and no one came. Exasperated, on the fourth
day, she took a postcard and hastily scribbled a message :
"Washing machine broke down. Send mechanic immediately." The very next day, before noon, a repairman
came. The woman could not understand the sudden

response. But when she inquired of the repairman why the slow response to her first letter and the instant reply to the second, he said, "When we read your first note, we thought that if you knew that much about the washing machine you should be able to fix it yourself. But when your second card came this morning we knew you needed help."

In the Epistle of James, the biblical letter which stresses faith and works, it is written:

> Is anyone among you suffering? He should keep on praying about it. And those who have reason to be thankful should continually be singing praises to the Lord. Is anyone sick? He should call for the elders of the church and they should pray over him and pour a little oil upon him, calling on the Lord to heal him. And their prayer, if offered in faith, will heal him, for the Lord will make him well; and if his sickness was caused by some sin, the Lord will forgive him. Admit your faults to one another and pray for each other so that you may be healed. The earnest prayer of a righteous man has great power and wonderful results (James 5:13-16).

The author of the Epistle makes it clear that the key to healing ministries is remembering that it is God who brings about the healing result. The prayer of faith is the recognition of God's power, the acknowledgment of human need, and the request for direct divine assistance. But invoking divine assistance should not be restricted to physical disabilities alone. Mental, emotional, spiritual, social, and interpersonal disorders, and even memories, need healing and wholeness. Whatever the setting, whatever the nature of the need, the person seeking assistance should be looking to God for deliverance, not to the human agent who prays the prayer of faith. Healing and wholeness may be sudden, or it may be slow in coming. Statistical success scores or attempts to document particular cures should not be the goal of the healing encounter. The aim is to center the attention of the faithful on the divine resource and to experience the liberating power of God. The result wll be manifest "in the fulness of time."

A noted surgeon, concerned about the statistical success scores of a certain widely known "healer," attempted to follow up on eighty-two persons who were allegedly healed at one of the services. Most of them were difficult to locate. But the doctor did succeed in interviewing twenty-three persons. According to his report, not one of them had been miraculously cured of anything. "Furthermore," he added, "these were people who still insisted that they had been cured, or they hedged and said they had been helped." Statistically oriented healers, who boast of instantaneous miraculous results, run the risk of inflating their numbers in order to draw larger and larger crowds. Or they may coerce those who come for help into pseudo-psychic healing without lasting effect. Or, even worse, they may increase the disability or bring about the death of ardent followers by encouraging them to give up immediately their medicine or other physical supports.

All healing is divine. The role of the physician and surgeon should always be included in the prayer of faith. God has given devoted health practitioners knowledge and skills which facilitate the healing process. Faith supplements and reinforces this procedure by helping the patient to see and experience God's power through all of the healing channels in the earth. The fact that Jesus mixed a mud pack to apply to the eyes of the blind man may be a suggestion in support of the role of the physician. Physicians can give medicines and surgeons can provide the skilled incision and suture, but all healing and wholeness finally is an act of God. More faith is needed in the doctor's office, and more doctors are needed in the houses of faith.

The healing of the soul is a more prevalent need than the healing of the body. Dr. William Glasser employs what he calls "reality therapy." He contends that the recovery of a mentally disturbed patient can be thwarted if the therapist permits the patient to blame all his or her difficulties on someone else. This "may make the patient feel good temporarily at the price of evading responsibility." Though the word "sin" is in disrepute, some therapists are beginning to believe that the significance of sin needs to be reinterpreted so that patients may confront their own wrongdoing honestly, admitting their fault. In some instances, only a sense of divine forgiveness can enable a soul-sick person to shake off the burden of depression and experience a new sense of freedom and release.

Deep-seated emotional illness, resulting from profound interpersonal conflict, can only be relieved when the tension resulting from hatred and estrangement is relieved. The awareness of God's goodness and love may be the only way that two hardened, hateful people can find the path which leads toward reconciliation, renewal, and personal peace.

Slumbering local churches must awaken to their spiritual potential. Each can become a mighty spiritual center for healing and wholeness in the community. Special services which include Bible reading, audible sharing of concerns, and prayer should also provide opportunities for persons to come forward for the "prayer of faith." The Sacrament of the Holy Communion, with its call to the faithful to come to the table, provides an excellent time for general and specific healing therapy. Each person may silently locate his or her own particular need and place that concern before the Lord as he or she eats the bread and drinks from the cup.

Individual counseling experiences can be spiritually enriched by closing such encounters with the laying on of hands and praying the prayer of faith. A visit to the sick, in home or in institution, can be greatly enriched by brief selected Bible readings and the prayer of faith. The careful art of laying on hands as the prayer is given adds meaning and transmits a message of human and divine concern. Not long ago in a visit to Southeast Asia, I noted the number of religious shrines scattered about the community. They were always open, and there were always people quietly enjoying private acts of personal devotion. But in most Western communities, the churches are closed. Roman Catholic churches have had a good tradition of the open door, still maintained in many places. But security problems have affected this ministry. Someone needs to be present in the open sanctuary, not simply because security is necessary, but also because many lonely people feel more at ease in a large strange church building when someone responsible is present.

Perhaps the next project for the ecumenical movement, at the local level, should be to open the doors of our churches. Now that we have overcome denominational pride and prejudice, perhaps the people of God are ready to support an "open door" church ministry. Not all of the churches would be opened every day. But certain churches, strategically located and beautifully designed, could be designated as places for prayer and meditation, open to whosoever will. Perhaps retired persons could be used as hosts so that someone would be present in the sanctuary from morning till dusk. A minister or priest could be assigned with posted hours on certain days of the week. This would provide those who need to share with someone an immediate opportunity to talk to a trained clergy person. The open churches could be advertised by special signs at each immediate location and wide publicity in newspapers and other media. Thus, local churches could become "spiritual sane asylums" where young and old could stop for rest and prayer. An ecumenical budget would be needed to share the costs, but this could be provided.

But building-centered ministries in institutional churches are not enough. It is always to be remembered that Jesus met and ministered to most of the people he assisted in the marketplace, along the highways, and in the places where the multitudes gathered. There are millions of people like the Gadarene demoniac, the woman at the well, the little child who wandered into the crowd, Mary and Martha mourning the death of Lazarus, blind Bartimaeus, the man at the Beautiful Gate of the temple, the daughter of the Syro-Phoenician woman, the ten lepers, and the thief on the cross—people whose faith will not be fully confirmed until they experience the healing power of God.

Distraught teen-agers, miserably married couples, the lonely rich, sullen prisoners, the indigent aging, the disillusioned activist, and the deserted poor, all need healing and wholeness. They are within reach of God's miraculous blessings if we are willing to stretch forth our hands toward them.

Chapter X

Diversity:
The Gift of God
I Corinthians 12:1

In addition to theological difficulties and disagreements, the apostolic church had at least two other big problems to resolve: racism and spiritual elitism. Jesus had given his disciples a clear target when he left them: "Go ye therefore, and teach all nations . . . all things whatsoever I have commanded you . . ." (Matthew 28:19-20). But it is to be remembered that Jesus gave this "great commission" to a group of Jewish disciples, men whose experience and learning was limited to a miniscule section of the world. Even though the Master's message had universal implications, Jesus himself during his earthly ministry never traveled beyond the boundaries of his own nation. Even after the resurrection, the missionary vision of the disciples was restricted to the land they knew best. Simon Peter announced that he would return to his old occupation, and the others, not knowing what else to do, decided to do likewise. Evidently, they intended to support themselves by working at regular tasks and share the good news of the gospel on a part-time basis.

Fifty days after the resurrection of Christ, the disciples had a meeting in the city of Jerusalem and were assembled for prayer and fellowship in a certain house, while they were experiencing an extraordinary period of unity, a spiritual explosion broke loose:

> ". . . a sound from heaven like the rushing of a violent wind, and it filled the house. . . . Before their eyes appeared tongues like flames, which separated off and settled above the head of each one of them. They were all filled with the Holy Spirit and began to speak in different languages as the Spirit gave them power to proclaim his message. (Acts 2:2-4 *Phillips*)

Travelers and business people from all of the nations round about, as far away as Egypt and Rome, were present in Jerusalem at the time. When they heard the commotion, they came to see what was happening. They were all amazed at what they saw and heard. Some asked, "What on earth does this mean?" Others laughed and accused the disciples of being drunk. Peter then stepped forward and addressed the crowd, saying, "These men are not drunk as you suppose. . . . No, this was predicted by the prophet Joel. . . . Men of Israel, I beg of you to listen to my words (Acts 2:22 *Phillips*). Then Peter preached the gospel to them. He declared that Jesus of Nazareth had proved by miracles and signs that he was sent from God. His crucifixion had been turned into victory, for the Lord had raised him from the dead.

Peter's message was addressed to an international, interracial congregation. This was the first time that such a varied group of people had heard the gospel. When Peter had finished speaking, several persons in the crowd shouted, "What shall we do now?" Peter called for repentance and confession of faith in Jesus Christ. Three thousand converts were baptized that day, and the character of the Christian movement was permanently changed.

The conversion of Saul, some time later, introduced another new ingredient into the widening ranks of the Christian community. Saul, whose name was later changed to Paul, was a native of Tarsus in Asia Minor. He was a Hellenistic Jew and a citizen of Rome. After his miraculous conversion, he spent some years in study and reflection. In response to the Macedonian vision, he decided to carry the gospel to Greece and Rome. Paul made three missionary journeys. Under his leadership the non-Jewish sector of the church increased. Soon the Jewish congregations in Jerusalem were a minority group. But because Jews were the first to hear the gospel and because Jesus and all of the first apostles were Jewish, Jews dominated the Jerusalem-centered congregations under the leadership of Simon Peter.

It was inevitable, however, that the growing diversity in the church would require special attention from its leadership. The first difficulty arose in the congregation at Jerusalem when certain Hellenists accused the Jews, who were handling most of the administrative matters, of discrimination in the distribution of assistance to the widows. After some discussion, an interracial committee of deacons was chosen to oversee the details of the fellowship and insure equal treatment for all.

Paul's missionary successes increased his influence in the church. He was careful, however, to maintain good relations with the church leaders at Jerusalem, including Simon Peter. But, as Paul's theological perspective began to take form, it was clear that problems were going to develop. The first issue that crystalized centered around the question of whether Gentile converts should be forced to obey all of the traditions common to the Jews, including circumcision. Apparently, this was the custom among the Petrine Christians who were largely of Jewish

origin. But in Paul's ministry to the Gentiles, he was
dealing with a constituency which had little awareness of
the traditions of the Jews. Furthermore, Paul was
preaching a gospel of freedom in Christ which fulfilled the
expectations of the old covenant and introduced a new
relationship to God. Justification by faith in the finished
work of Christ superseded the old requirements.
Therefore, Paul contended, Gentile converts should not
be burdened with the religious practices of Judaism.

At first, Simon Peter was opposed to this point of view.
But later developments clearly indicate that Simon's
position changed on this matter. He perceived that, even
though he was emotionally related to the traditions of the
past, Paul's missionary endeavor was being blessed by
God and that the church was growing in strength day by
day as a result of Paul's diligence. Furthermore, it seemed
evident that Peter was moved by Paul's theological
interpretations. In fact, in the sermon at Pentecost, Peter
himself seemed to be anticipating Paul's doctrines.
Finally, the issue was resolved in a great conference in
Jerusalem. Peter's brilliant defense of Paul's ministry, in
spite of the objections of the conservative Jewish church
leaders, led to the endorsement of Paul's preaching.

Paul was officially committed to spread the gospel
among the Gentiles, but the Jewish assemblage adopted
some basic restrictions. All Christians were to abstain
from eating meat offered to idols, the drinking of animal
blood, the eating of meat that had been strangled, and
from sexual immorality.

But as Paul moved from city to city establishing new
congregations, controversies began to emerge. So it
became necessary for the apostle to write letters to the
young Christians to set them straight on issues critical to a
proper understanding of the faith. Paul had at least four

major responsibilities in stabilizing the rapidly growing Christian community. The first was helping his new converts to get a clear and proper understanding of the theology of the new faith. Secondly, in the face of the libertine practices of the Greco-Roman world which surrounded them, it was necessary to establish Christian ethics and morality in the life of the new converts. Thirdly, because the churches were composed of a racial and cultural mixture, mostly from the ranks of the poor, Paul had to deal with human pride and prejudice. Fourthly, since the early church was so consciously preoccupied with spiritual empowerment, the apostle had to watch for the ever-encroaching divisiveness of spiritual elitism.

In his beautiful letter to the Ephesian congregation, Paul said:

> Make it your aim to be at one in the Spirit, and you will inevitably be at peace with one another. You all belong to one Body, of which there is one Spirit, just as you all experienced one calling to one hope. There is one Lord, one faith, one baptism, one Father of us all, who is the one over all, the one working through all and the one living in all. Naturally, there are different gifts and functions; individually grace is given to us in different ways out of the rich diversity of Christ's giving. (4:1-7 *Phillips*)

On another occasion Paul found it necessary to write to the Christians in Corinth. He had considerable difficulty with them. Some had taken up life styles of their own choosing, in the name of Christian liberty, and Paul took them to task with strong language. In the twelfth chapter of First Corinthians, however, Paul seems to be dealing with efforts on the part of some of the members to establish certain priorities among themselves according to spiritual rank. They were designating certain kinds of ministry more important than others, thus implying some differentiation on God's part in the distribution of spiritual gifts and graces. But Paul explained to the young Christians that God works through different persons in different ways, it is the same Spirit that inspires and empowers.

> Each person is given his/her gift by the Spirit that he/she may use it for the common good . . . of all. Some may have more knowledge; others may seem to be wiser; still others may manifest greater faith; some may be gifted at healing; others at the ability to do great deeds; some may have the gift of prophecy, while others are distinguished preachers. Others may be more sensitive in matters of spiritual discernment. Some may speak in tongues, while others may be able to interpret. . . . But behind all of these gifts is the operation of the same Spirit. (12:4-7)

Then the apostle goes on to utter a classic statement concerning the nature of the church, comparing it to the body:

> As the human body, which has many parts, is a unity, and those parts despite their multiplicity constitute one single body . . .whether we are Jews, Gentiles, slaves or free men . . . we have all had experience of the same Spirit. . . . So that the eye cannot say to the hand "I don't need you." nor, again, can the head say to the feet, "I don't need you." (I Corinthians 12:12-21 *Phillips*)

This translation gives vividness to Paul's utterance. The parts (of the body) which do not look beautiful have a deeper beauty in the work they do, while the parts which look beautiful may not be at all essential to life! But God has harmonized the whole body by giving importance of function to the parts . . . that the body should work together as a whole with all the members in sympathetic relationship with one another. So it happens that if one member suffers all the other members suffer with it, and if one member is honored all the members share a common joy (I Corinthians 12:23-26).

The overwhelming intentionality in the Epistles of Paul would seem to label pluralism in the church a heresy. "Pluralism" is a term which may properly be applied to a nation with many geographically, racially, or culturally defined groups. Each has a right to be different, and even separate, if they choose. They may have different religious loyalties and language. But the world-wide Christian church, under God, is a covenantal community of faith and good works inaugurated by Jesus Christ and constituted of persons of many races, colors, and cultures, many talents and ministries. But we are committed to each other in a very peculiar fashion because individually and collectively we are one body in Christ!

What does all this mean to contemporary Christianity? In a world where national and ideological differences continue to threaten peace; where racial and cultural presumptions are demanding first priority; where elitism of every sort threatens to erode efforts at unity, the church of Jesus Christ must hold forth a redeeming message of unity in Christ. All of our identities are legitimate and God-given, deserving respect. But the genius of the Christian community is to express our several beauties together. This is not a call for a merger or sublimation of our several distinctions and dignities, but rather an opportunity to unite them all in the common task of saving the world from the sin of separateness.

In the church of Jesus Christ, no one is free to choose a life-style inconsistent with the expectations of Jesus as set forth in the Scripture. No person or group is free to separate from the rest of us in the name of race, culture, spiritual, or secular elitism. We are together trying to express a new identity in which our differences are mutually yoked so that all members "share a common joy."

Some years ago Daniel Poling wrote a rather pessimistic book entitled, *The Last Years of the Church.* He saw the church in its present form failing—closing its doors in changing neighborhoods, unable to cope with the diversity of race. He saw the church polarized in its inability to take sides on clear issues of justice over against oppression. He saw the church conducting its one-hour-a-week worship ceremony then forgetting about the world the rest of the time. He saw the church disinterestedly mouthing the old slogans of salvation but neglecting the work of salvation in the world.

His pessimism would be totally justified if it were not for the hopeful sign of renewed churches across the country and the world who are seriously addressing themselves to the task of fulfilling the missional requirements of Jesus. Wherever such churches have turned their attention toward their communities and the world with need-serving compassionate ministries, there has been an enthusiastic response on the part of the people.

As the Christian church closes the last of the twentieth century and looks toward the twenty-first, it must recogize that the ordained clergy alone cannot effectively carry the gospel message to the world, using the old models we have employed for so long. The pulpit and the pew must close ranks.

Lay persons must once again become involved in every aspect of ministry. Systematic training experiences must be inaugurated by every segment of the church to instruct the laity in all of the functions of ministry. Lay persons must master the art of visiting the sick, attending the prisoner, empowering the poor. Lay persons must be prepared for critical leadership roles involving the great issues of justice and fair play as they relate to business, labor unions, education, politics, economics, and the organizational life of groups of every kind. Lay persons themselves must become the integral catalysts in penetrating every segment of the life of the community and nation with the demands of the gospel of Jesus Christ, seven days a week. Lay persons must master the capability to do crisis counseling and referral, since they encounter many people in their daily vocations who need immediate and mature conversation. Lay persons must learn to witness intelligently to the truth of the gospel, so they may effectively engage their companions in religious dialogue. Lay persons must increase as ministerial assistants in every local church. Lay persons must become proficient in Bible teaching and doing theology so that the multiplied power of the church of Jesus Christ may be felt in a sustaining way all of the time, everywhere on earth. Lay persons must accept full responsibility for the moral and ethical character of the community.

The people of God have been endowed with a diversity of gifts and graces. Now we must apply all of our talents in carrying the whole gospel to the whole world.

Chapter XI

Sufficient Grace
II Corinthians 12:9

When families sit around a common table, bow their heads and touch hands in an act of prayer, we call it table grace. It is usually a time of thanksgiving for the food and a request for God's blessing upon it and upon those who have gathered to break bread. Grace is sometimes used to describe a person who possesses unusual charm, or one whose courteous manner deserves commendation. Legally, a "grace period" is the extension of a deadline to pay a debt or some other previously agreed upon obligation. But in Christian theological usage, grace expresses the church's most distinctive and important doctrine. It was St. Paul's personal religous awakening and his later reflections and writings which produced this extraordinary understanding of the nature of God.

The word "grace" itself is related to the Greek word *charis*. The Greeks used *charis* to translate the Hebrew word for "favor;" as, for example, "favor in the eyes of God." Paul's knowledge of his Jewish heritage and his expertise in linguistic usage may have contributed to his own theological formulation with reference to grace.

Paul was a Pharisee who was thoroughly convinced that the Christians were misguided blasphemers, the enemies of God. The first New Testament mention of the unconverted Saul finds him with a group of Jewish zealots in the act of stoning the apostle Stephen to death. This was probably not Saul's first or his last execution. Some time later, on the road to Damascus, on one of his missions of death, a bright light from above blinded Saul. His horse reared and Saul was thrown to the ground. As he groveled in the dust, trying to understand what had happened, he heard a voice saying, "Saul, Saul, why persecutest thou me?" Saul responded, "Who art thou Lord?" The voice answered, "I am Jesus whom thou persecutest." Then Saul cried out: "Lord, what wilt thou have me to do?" (Acts 9:4-6).

From that moment Saul's life was changed. He began to associate himself with the Christians, even though he was treated with suspicion by some who were not convinced of the credibility of his conversion. But he was befriended by a Christian leader named Ananias in Damascus. Afterward, Saul spent an extended period in study and reflection. The Christians changed his name to Paul, and soon his remarkable energy and passion were harnessed to the task of proclaiming the gospel of Christ. He joined himself to Barnabas and together they went everywhere preaching the word of God.

The Damascus experience and the life transformation that followed had a profound affect on Paul's theology. Later, in a letter to one of his congregations in Corinth, he said, "I am the least worthy of all the apostles, and I shouldn't even be called an apostle at all after the way I treated the church of God. But whatever I am now it is all because God poured out such kindness and grace upon me" (I Corinthians 15:9-10 *LB*). And in a letter to the church at Rome, he makes explicit his emerging theology: "And now, through Christ, all the kindness of God has been poured out upon us undeserving sinners; and now he is sending us out around the world to tell all people everywhere the great things God has done for them, so that they, too, will believe and obey" (1:5 *LB*). Conscious of his guilt and unworthiness, Paul saw God's gift of forgiveness and his appointment as an apostle as a totally undeserved blessing. Overcome by the awareness of God's goodness, Paul seized upon the notion of grace to express his new-found understanding of the nature of God.

Paul connected his concept of grace to the cross:

> God showed his great love for us by sending Christ to die for us while we were still sinners. And since by his blood he did all this for us sinners, how much more will he do for us now that he has declared us not guilty? Now he will save us from all of God's wrath to come. And since, when we were his enemies, we were brought back to God by the death of his Son, what blessings he must have for us now that we are his friends, and he is living within us!" (Romans 5:8-10 *LB*).

Thus, the focal point of God's display of grace Paul interpreted as subsuming all of the expectations of the ancient sacrificial system of the Jews. In one act of grace upon the cross, not only does Christ save guilty sinners from the wrath of God, but through the means of grace those who receive the gift of God's salvation are also empowered to live a victorious life.

Beyond liberal and conservative theological controversies concerning Paul's interpretation of the meaning of the death of Christ, the apostle states a truth that is larger than theological differences: Christ is, above all else, a demonstration of the love of God. Christ actualizes the love of God. The work of Christ is the work of grace. This became the central note of deliverance in Paul's message to the world.

The two great passages which spell out the theological core of Paul's discovery are to be found in his letter to the Christians at Ephesus:

> And now God can always point to us as examples of how very, very rich his kindness is, as shown in all he has done for us through Jesus Christ. Because of his kindness you have been saved through trusting Christ. And even trusting is not of yourselves; it too is a gift from God. Salvation is not a reward for the good we have done, so none of us can take any credit for it. It is God himself who has made us what we are and given us new lives from Christ Jesus. . . . He planned that we should spend these lives in helping others." (2:7-10 *LB*)

This latter emphasis of Paul's builds into the theology of grace a social dimension which cannot be ignored. Since God has graciously extended divine deliverance to each of us, though we have done nothing to deserve it, we are inclined to express in word and deed the same graceful love and service toward our fellow human beings who suffer spiritual, political, or economic bondage.

Grace is the expression of the essence of God, whose nature and being is love. Faith is the enabling response of the believer who thus receives this gift. God's grace is an undeserved and unmerited gift. Grace actualizes the experience of God's love in the life of human beings.

There are some Old Testament references to the mercy of God which seem to foreshadow the New Testament conception of grace. But nowhere else in religious or secular literature is Paul's comprehension of the grace of God duplicated or superseded. Basically, Paul's spiritual insight gives us a new beginning in the search for divine understanding. Others have interpreted the spiritual quest as if human beings were seeking God, but Paul's illuminating interpretation of grace suggests that God is in pursuit of us.

St. Paul has four big words in his theological vocabulary: sin, grace, justification, and faith. Sin is the willful thought or action of a person that is contrary to the revealed will of God. Grace is the actualization of God's love in the world. It is the evidence of God's desire to forgive, redeem, and reconcile. Justification is the transaction of redemption, through Christ, whereby the sinner is restored to divine favor. And faith is the act of individual acceptance of God's graceful gift of forgiveness and a reconciliation. St. Augustine, one of the African theological giants of the early church, was a great advocate of the centrality of grace in Christian theology. Like Paul, he had a personal experience of divine deliverance from a life of sin and disobedience. His gratitude to God was overwhelming. Augustine felt undeserving. Nothing he had done merited God's goodness. This filled his whole being with a deep desire to express his appreciation to God with a life of faithful service.

But with the developmental history of institutional Christianity in the West, the reassertion of the legalistic requirements of the old covenant became more and more a precondition to salvation. The church, posssessing the keys, became the bursar of all of the benefits of God. Rules and regulations were fixed to determine eligibility, and the arbitrary authority of the heirarchy obscured the original Pauline interpretation of grace. More and more, good works, obedience to the prescribed dictums of the church, and the arbitrary pronouncements of popes and councils dominated the life and experience of the believer.

Reformation Protestant theologians resurrected Pauline theology, restoring to the church an interpretation of good works as the fruit of a grateful life rather than an effort to merit the favor of God. And Luther gave renewed emphasis to Paul's great phrases, "By grace are ye saved through faith, and that not of yourselves: it is a gift of God: not of works lest any man should boast" (Ephesians 5:8-9). From the fifth chapter of Romans, Luther revived Paul's central doctrine: "Therefore being justified by faith, we have peace with God through our Lord Jesus Christ: by whom also we have access by faith into this grace wherein we stand" (verse 1).

The great ages of evangelistic excitement in the life of the church have always been associated with a renewed emphasis on the grace of God. The unbeliever is stirred not only by the fact of the love of God but by the notion that the pursuing grace of God in Jesus Christ intensifies that love. To discover that we are loved and aggressively pursued by God ignites a warming glow of gratitude, making it possible for us not only to love God but to enthusiastically love each other.

Love is learned behavior. Love cannot be fully given until it is fully received. To receive God's love makes possible a personal empowerment whose redemptive influence is strong enough to change our lives, renew our marriages, transform our homes, rebuild our broken friendships, and save the world.

Efforts have been made to study the applications of God's grace and describe its work in particular situations. But, at best, these attempts provide an opportunity to appreciate the many ways in which God's love relates to the life of the world. John Wesley, for example, gave considerable thought to what he called "prevenient grace," which is the notion that God is actively reaching out toward unbelievers, preparing them to respond to divine love. Evangelists speak of "saving grace," which is the act of God which converts and transforms the soul. "Sanctifying grace" in the Roman Catholic theology is similar to what charismatics call "the gift of the Holy Spirit."

But all of these designations only sharpen the significance of the biblical admonition: "Grow in grace, and in the knowledge of our Lord and Savior Jesus Christ" (II Peter 3:18). Growing in grace is an invitation to develop, to a higher point of sensitivity, our perception of the many ways in which the love of God is actualized in our lives and in the life of the world. This is precisely what was happening in the life of St. Paul. He was discovering that God's grace, expressed in Jesus Christ, was not a one-time experience; but, through the action of God's Holy Spirit, grace continues to bless and strengthen the life of faith and good works forever.

The great apostle had a problem. He was plagued by what he called "a thorn in the flesh" which troubled him. We do not know precisely the nature of Paul's affliction. Some think it might have been recurring epilepsy. Others say eye trouble was the source of his discomfort. Still others conjecture that it might have been malaria, but no one really knows. It might have been the "thorn" that troubles you and me. Paul spent three long seasons in prayer, requesting that he be healed and made rid of his ailment. But the only answer forthcoming from God was:

My strength is made perfect in weakness. Most gladly therefore will I rather glory in my infirmities, that the power of Christ may rest upon me. Therefore I take pleasure in (my) infirmities, in reproaches, in necessities, in persecutions, in distresses for Christ's sake: for when I am weak, then I am strong (II Corinthians 12:9-10).

Paul, then, interpreted his difficulty as an irritant to keep him humble. His disability, he declared, added more glory to God and reduced his own pridefulness. His courageous testimony has a timeless value:

The sufficiency of grace is testimony to the infinite capacity of God's all-encompassing love. Paul's discovery gives encouragement to all who must live with the discomfort of some "thorn in the flesh." Instead of a life of condemnation to painful humiliation and frustration, we have another choice: victory through the empowering sufficiency of the grace of God. The Living Bible has a lucid and inspiring translation of Paul's testimony to the church at Rome and Corinth:

Nothing can ever separate us from his love. Death can't, and life can't. The angels won't, and all of the power of hell itself cannot keep God's love away (Romans 8:38).

We are pressed on every side by troubles, but not crushed and broken. We are perplexed because we don't know why things happen as they do, but we don't give up and quit. . . . God never abandons us. We get knocked down, but we get up again and keep going. . . . Our inner strength in the Lord is growing every day (II Corinthians 8-9, 16).

Thanks be to God, which giveth us the
Victory through our Lord Jesus Christ.

Chapter XII

No More Sea
Revelation 21:1

In the Aegean Sea, southwest of the city of Ephesus and just off the coat of Asia minor, there is an island called Patmos. It has a place in biblical history because it was here that the revelation of John took form. John had been isolated on the island by the Roman government as a penalty for teaching the gospel of Jesus Christ. It all happened during the reign of the Emperor Domitian, who ruled the Roman Empire between A.D. 81 and 96. His years of power were difficult times for the Christians. The fact that John was placed on Patmos as a prisoner suggests that he must have been an influential and highly respected Christian leader. The government was afraid to dispose of him, so isolation on Patmos became the next best alternative.

Three centuries of intermittent persecution characterized the early years of the church's history. Then, in the fourth century, the Emperor Constantine became a Christian convert. Through his initiative, Christianity, which had been an outlaw religion, suddenly became the official religion of the Roman Empire. Not only did Constantine join the church, but he commanded all of his soldiers and his courtiers to do likewise. But beneath his new-found piety there was a practical political purpose for changing his attitude toward Christianity. Christianity had become the most influential single movement in the empire. Rome was having trouble. Constantine needed the cohesive potential of Christianity to consolidate the empire's sprawling dominion.

But in the first century when John received his revelation on the Isle of Patmos, Christians were classified as enemies of Rome. There were at least three distinct reasons why the Roman government distrusted the church. First of all, the Christians were opposed to emperor worship. Imperial shrines were located in all of the principal cities. But bowing down to the statue of an emperor was contrary to Christian teaching. The Mosaic law, with its strong emphasis upon the singular sovereignty of God and its warning against all forms of imagery and idolatry, was deeply ingrained in Christian conscience. Because the Christians refused to obey the imperial commands to venerate the statues of the emperor, they were suspected of being disloyal. All this was complicated by the fact that the Christians refused to enlist for military service. Secondly, the Christians preached the coming kingdom of God. The trial of Jesus, which led to his conviction and death, had centered attention on Christian goals, especially the notion of the coming of the kingdom of God. There was always suspicion on the part of the Roman government that this spiritualized Christian expectation was a cover-up for more subtle operations and intentions. After all, in times past the Romans had contended with attempts on the part of the Jews to foment revolution. The third concern was the simple fact that the Christians were growing in number. At first their influence was primarily among the poor, but gradually persons from all walks of life began to respond to the new faith.

To be a Christian in those early days was risky. But in spite of the dangers the church grew. Dr. Jan Lochman, a professor at the University of Basil in Switzerland, wrote an article some time ago entitled, "Christians Without Privileges." He described the difficulties under which the churches were laboring in those sections of the world now under the domination of Marxist governments. Though public policy makes religious discrimination illegal, Christans definitely experience discouragement. Their children have greater difficulty in gaining entrée to training for the sensitive professions which might result in their becoming leaders, supervisors, or managers. Even though Christians may possess superior abilities, totalitarian states still distrust Chistianity's spiritual dynamics.

But in spite of the impediments, Dr. Lochman points out, Christians behind the Iron Curtain are rediscovering the deeper meaning of their faith and deciding to accept the disadvantages involved in professing their faith rather than forsaking the church and surrendering their discipleship. Without privileges, these Christians persist. The communist expectation that the church would disappear in a generation has met with disappointment. On the contrary, the churches are stronger.

The Christians of the first century experienced daily persecution, harassment, and death. But the more Rome resisted the new religion, the more heroic the Christians became. It was in such an atmosphere of hostility that the word of the Lord came to John on the island of Patmos. The written record of God's disclosures are included in a little book called The Revelation of John. When John's Patmos message reached the suffering Christians, it lifted their morale. Above all else it gave the assurance that

God was still involved in this period of their despair and that history was not running loose, beyond divine control.

There had grown up in the early church the teaching that Jesus would return in power and glory before the apostles died. On one occasion, when Jesus was sharing with his disciples the words concerning his death, he said, "And some of you standing right here now will certainly live to see me coming in my Kingdom" (Matthew 16:28 *LB*). The Second Epistle of Peter bears testimony to the fact that Christians were being taunted by skeptics who were inquiring, "So Jesus promised to come back, did he? Then where is he? He'll never come" (3:4 *LB*). So after all of the original apostles had died, the apprehension of doubters increased. John's revelation was an answer to that dilemma. He begins with this word of explanation:

> "This book unveils some of the future activities soon to occur in the life of Jesus Christ. God permitted him to reveal these things to his servant John in a vision; and then an angel was sent from heaven to explain the vision's meaning. . . . If you read this prophesy aloud to the church, you will receive a special blessing from the Lord. Those who listen to it being read and do what it says will be blessed. The time is near when these things will come true. (Revelation 1:1-3 *LB*)

Genesis, the first book of the Bible, is the book of beginnings. Its author gives a clear and simple statement of God's creative actions. On the other hand, The Revelation, the last book of the Bible, is cloaked in mystery. Rome is referred to as Babylon. Aside from specific mention of the names of the churches in Asia Minor, all references are masked in picturesque symbolism. The content of the book is divided into three parts.

The first three chapters deal with the message to the contemporary churches. Chapters 4 to 20 set forth the impending judgments of God. Chapters 21 and 22 describe God's new beginnings after the final judgment.

The messages to the seven churches located in Asia Minor are quite specific. In each instance an angel is designated to bear the word of the Lord to the congregations. Two phrases dominate the rhythmic recital of God's oracles. The first is, "I know thy works" (cf. Revelation 2:2). This is the divine reminder of the all-seeing eye of God. God knows whether we are really carrying forth the business of the kingdom or simply developing institutional churches adapted to our own tastes and desires. "I know thy works" could be considered bad news for fraudulent congregations. But the good news is that it is nice to be known best by the One who loves us most. Even though all of the churches fell short of God's expectations, they were not deserted. God was ready to restore and empower the churches, if the congregations were willing.

The second recurring phrase is, "He that hath an ear to hear, let him hear what the Spirit saith unto the churches" (cf. Revelation 2:7). This is a clear call to the Christians to interpret wisely God's message and to reorder their agenda according to God's instruction.

The church at Ephesus was commended for hard work and patience and their resistance to religious fakers. But, on the other hand, they were chided for letting their spiritual sensitiveness grow dull. They had a lot of activity going, but their consciousness of Christ as the living head of the church had faded. The city of Smyrna had a temple to Tiberius and another to the goddess Roma. Hence, the Christians there were under great pressure. The Smyrna congregation was poor in this world's goods, but God declared them spiritually rich because they were faithful to the gospel. However, they did have in their midst some pretenders—salamander Christians, using subterfuges to keep their identity hidden so they would not be called upon to make an open stand for Christ.

Pergamos was characterized as "Satan's seat" because the city had temples to Zeus, Athena, Dionysius, Augustus, and Roma. This made it extremely difficult for the Christians to resist coercion into idolatry. Furthermore, a sect in the church called the Nicolaitans was teaching compromise on the issue of emperor worship and encouraging Christians to buy meat offered to idols because it was cheap. Thyatira had a good ministry to the poor and a reputation for love and faith, but her Christian integrity had been eroded by compromises. The church located in the city of Sardis needed a revival.

The Philadelphia congregation received extraordinary commendation because it was striving to preach and practice the whole gospel of Jesus Christ, in word and deed, but some of the members didn't like it. They preferred the old-time religion, with its emphasis on one part of the gospel and the neglect of other parts. To the Philadelphians, God said, "Behold, I have set before thee an open door, and no man can shut it" (Revelation 3:8). But the church at Laodicea received a stinging rebuke because it was lukewarm, and uncommitted, popular but unfaithful. In disgust, the angel of the Lord said, "I will spew thee out of my mouth" (Revelation 3:16).

These are timeless messages, addressed to the ancient churches in Asia Minor. But the incisive words of the Lord might well be tested against the profile of the local churches of our time. What would the angel of the Lord say after close examination of our stewardship in the church to which we belong? Would the words of commendation overshadow the criticisms? Every governing board of every local church needs to confront the angel of the Lord and redirect the energy of its congregation according to the directives of Jesus Christ.

In verse six of the fourth chapter, there is a description of the universe. It reflects the view of the ancient Hebrews. Earth and heaven are divided from each other by the firmament, the sky. But above the firmament, there is a great sea which separates earth from heaven. From above, God can see what is going on below; but the crystal barrier symbolizes the estrangement between God and the creatures of the earth. Suddenly the impending judgments of God against the persistent opposition of Rome breaks lose. Trumpets sound. Scrolls unfold. Books are opened. Voices speak. Horrible agents of divine wrath surge forth. The succeeding chapters reveal one startling happening after another. Strange creatures perform the awful duties of destruction. Each terrible episode of judgment introduces another until finally, in one great act of God, evil is permanently defeated. Peace without interruption becomes possible. So chapter 21 opens with these beautiful words of John: "And I saw a new heaven and a new earth: for the first heaven and the first earth were passed away: and there was no more sea." The Living Bible has an interesting translation of the remainder of the passage:

> And I, John, saw the Holy City, the new Jerusalem, coming down from God out of heaven. It was a glorious sight, beautiful as a bride at her wedding. I heard a loud shout from the throne saying, "Look, the home of God is now among men, and he will live with them and they will be his people; yes, God himself will be among them. He will wipe away all tears from their eyes, and there shall be no more death, nor sorrow, nor crying, nor pain. All of

that has gone forever." And the one sitting on the throne said, "See, I am making all things new!" (Revelation 21:2-5)

The statement "and there was no more sea" has deep significance. It corresponds to the description in the fourth chapter of the Revelation. The "sea" had been a barrier, separating the creator from the creatures. Now this sea of glass is gone forever. Nothing is left to restrict or encumber the freedom of fellowship between God and the people of God.

No portrayal of the blissful reward of the righteous could be more beautifully set forth. John sees the end of sorrow, death, and pain. It is interesting, however, that the celestial community, as described in The Revelation, is a city, not a garden like the original dwelling place of Adam and Eve as described in Genesis. And the city has twelve gates—three on the east, north, west, and south—so the faithful coming from all directions have easy access. A river with beautiful trees growing on its banks flows through the center of this divine paradise, and the leaves of the trees are for the healing of the nations. There is no temple or place of worship, for the abiding presence of God has replaced all substitutes. The curse, sin, is gone forever, so that the possibility of failure is no longer present. And there is no night. The presence of God gives eternal light. And the gates of the city are always open, for the danger of corruption within or without has been permanently removed.

Then, as if to add a reassuring benediction to those who have suffered through so many disappointments, John adds, "Nothing unclean, no one who deals in filthiness and lies, shall ever at any time enter it (the city)—only those whose names are written in the Lamb's book of life (Revelation 21:27 *Phillips*).

Every living religion has its own version of the "blessed hope," a final reward for the faithful. Perhaps there should be added to the list of expressions of God's grace a place for what I would call "eschatological grace." The word "eschatology" means "the doctrine of the end." "Eschatological grace" is the doctrine of the new beginning. It is the prospect which keeps the spirit of expectancy alive in the church. The people of God are always looking for the coming kingdom.

In faithfulness to the Great Commission of Christ, we are always preparing the way for that kingdom. But the consummation of all we hope for, in the end, comes to pass through the mighty action of God. In the beginning all things were created by the words and the works of God; so, in the end, all things are redeemed and permanently renewed by the words and deeds of God. And the angel of the Lord said, "Behold, I come quickly" (Revelation 22:7).

Thanks be to God, which giveth us the victory through our Lord Jesus Christ.

Chapter XIII

Let's Move . . .
Matthew 28:19

Jesus gave his disciples a great commission before he left the earth: "Go ye therefore, and teach all nations, baptizing them in the name of the Father, and of the Son, and of the Holy Ghost (Matthew 28:19). Our task is clear: to carry the message of Christ, in word and deed, to the whole wide world. The size of that responsibility is growing. Everyday 210,000 new people are born: every week, 1.5 million; every month, 6.5 million; and every year, 76 million—enough to populate a country the size of East and West Germany combined. The implication of these figures escalates the mandate of Jesus from urgency to emergency status. Some will ask, Why should we be worried about carrying the Christian witness to all these people? Is it because mainline American denominations have lost heavily in the last decade? Are we motivated by a purely selfish institutional survival interest? If so, our pursuit of people disgraces the name of Jesus Christ.

Christian missionaries have succeeded in planting the seeds of Christianity everywhere on earth. In the West, however, secularism has dulled the "two-edged sword" of the gospel and reduced our sense of urgency. Preoccupied with the immediacies of affluence, Christian evangelistic zeal has diminished. Marxist states declared religion "the opiate of the people," discouraging and restricting church development and outlawing what they call "religious propaganda." A new brand of "liberation theology" is challenging traditional Christianity in South America. Asian Christian communities are facing the resurgence of traditional non-Christian religions and government tendencies to brand Christianity as "foreign." Africa, south of the Sahara, is experiencing accelerated church growth, offering Christianity its most promising opportunity.

The stronger Western churches can help the struggling Christian communities in other parts of the world most effectively by providing money, personnel, and material assistance to train indigenous Christian leadership and strengthen indigenous Christian institutions. In the immediate foreseeable future, it seems likely that more restrictions will be placed upon "foreign missionaries." Hence, the major responsibility in the evangelization of people on the world's six continents depends upon the adequacy and preparation of indigenous lay and clergy leadership. In the face of this challenge, the missionary endeavor of the stronger churches must be increased, intensified and extended with the involvement of long- and short-term personnel and generous amounts of new money to support persons in mission and to develop indigenous Christian educational institutions.

We carry the message of Christ to all people everywhere because we believe not only that the grace of God revealed in Jesus Christ holds the promise of improving the quality of one's life, but also through Christ God gives deliverance from both the power and the penalty of sin. Our evangelism is an invitation to a new life in which justice and righteousness prevail. Authentic Christian evangelism is not a bigoted denunciation of men and women of other faiths. Rather, it is the proclamation of the latest edition of God's good news.

John Wesley's view of God's prevenient grace is a perennial safeguard against religious chauvinism. Wesley took seriously the universal implications of John 3:16:

> No man living is entirely destitute of what is vulgarly called "natural conscience"; but this is not natural; it is more properly termed "preventing (prevenient) grace. . . ." Everyone, unless he be one of the small number whose conscience is seared as with a hot iron, feels more or less uneasy when he acts contrary to the light of his own conscience. . . . So that no man sins because he hath not grace, but because he does not use the grace he hath.

In the Tuohy Lectures, Dr. Carl E. Braaten observed that it "is possible for a church to cease to be a church, to lose the gospel, to cool off . . . to become secularized to the point of being nothing more than an imitation of the world." Then he goes on to add:

> The Christian faith has a particular content. It makes a particular claim to truth, and that is that the all fulfilling future of mankind and of the world's salvation has already arrived in its initial phase in Jesus, the Jew from Nazareth. Any church that ceases to affirm this event and to live out its meaning has ceased to be a Christian community.

The 1972 United Methodist Doctrinal Statement in *The Book of Discipline* sets forth these clear words of witness:

> At the heart of the gospel of salvation is God's self-presentation (self-disclosure) in Jesus of Nazareth. Scripture focuses on the witness of Jesus' life and teachings, his death and resurrection, and his triumph within and over the agonies of history. Those who even now find in him their clue to God's redeeming love also

also find their hearts and wills transformed. In his life we see the power and wisdom of God, confirming his new covenant with his people in the revelation of the fullness of human possibilities. (1976 ed., par. 69)

Evangelism, ministry, and *mission* are one expression of the same threefold task of the church, as indivisibly joined as the trinitarian description of the Godhead. *Evangelism* is proclaiming that Jesus Christ has come into the world. This message must be declared with utter clarity and in a form that will capture the attention of every person who will listen. The object is to persuade persons to receive Christ's salvation, confess their faith, unite with a Christian fellowship, and live out the Master's discipleship requirement in the world.

The proclamation of the word must be skillfully directed. For example, while new confessions of faith are a top priority, the retrieving of dropouts is of equal importance. Then there is the need to arouse nominal Christians to reorder their lives with new and specific life dedication to some particular task or mission.

Also, the message must be directed toward skeptics, critics, and honest doubters, dealing carefully and sympathetically with their unreadiness and their intellectual and emotional resistances. Paul's skill and candor in approaching the skeptical at Mars' Hill is a model of good gospel communication worthy of imitation (Acts 17:22 ff.).

Ministry is the nurturing function in the Christian fellowship, local church, or parish. It is an educational engagement using all of the accoutrements of sound pedagogy. A church that is faithful to the gospel helps people to grow. John Wesley was peculiarly affected by the command of Jesus, "Be ye therefore perfect, even as your Father in heaven is perfect" (Matthew 5:48). Wesley considered it to be the will of God that his converts grow toward perfection, an achievement in "scriptural holiness," relentless pursuit of excellence in love. In one carefully considered statement he wrote:

> Neither dare we affirm as some have done, that all this salvation is given at once. There is indeed an instantaneous as well as a gradual work of God in his children. . . . There is a gradual work in the soul. . . . A long time, even many years, before sin is destroyed. . . . So that one may affirm the work is gradual; another is instantaneous, without any manner of contradiction.

Wesley's societies were designed to cultivate the growth of the people toward the improvement of their gifts and graces in every way. Evangelism anticipates growth. The alternative to growth is death. In response to the command and content of the gospel of Jesus Christ, the church must go and grow and give and do or die!

Mission is accepting the obligation and implementing the methodology which effectively carries the message of the whole gospel to the whole world. It is a traveling assignment in response to the Great Commission to win converts to the faith. Mission is directing the energies of growing Christians into channels of Christian witness and service; investing the power of the faithful into the never-ending struggle against evil; keeping unsoiled the frail garment of individual human dignity; improving mutual respect and relations between persons; challenging un-christian objectives, policies, organizations, and systems in the public and private sector; and explicitly confronting "the powers that be" whenever the exercise of their authority threatens that sensitive orbit of individual human freedoms and liberties given by God.

During the gas shortage of World War II, the government raised the constant question, "Is this trip necessary?" Today, inquirers are asking the same question with reference to Christianity. Is Christianity that important to the lives of human beings? Should the church be compulsively engaged in missionary enterprises in distant places? A 1978 Gallup Poll survey offered a partial reply. It reported that less than 28 percent of the persons interviewed, all of whom lived in the so-called Christian nations of the Western world, said that religion was not "very important" in their lives, though many more of these same people professed a vague belief in a supreme being.

Dr. Edward Norman, an eminent Anglican historian and a firm believer in traditional Christianity, in the 1978 London Reith Lectures declared, "The present decline of Christianity in the developed world (Western) is not the result of the assault of its enemies; but to its surrender of its unique claims to an understanding of the nature of men." He goes on to add that the waning power of the church is due to the fact that it has lost sight of its roots. He alleges that the church's moral idealism has forfeited transcendence in exchange for what he calls a "secularized mind." He then goes on to take a bold shot at what he alludes to as "the politicization of the clergy": "They have allowed themselves . . . to define their religious values according to categories and references provided by the compulsive moralism of contemporary intellectual culture." Dr. Norman's one-sided criticism deserves a hearing, even though I thoroughly reject the notion that Hebrew-Christian religion should keep away from so-called secular issues. How can one read the Bible and recall Moses' confrontation with the Pharaoh. Isaiah's total involvement in the politics of his time, Nathan's challenge to King David, Elijah's resistance to Ahab, Jesus' criticism of the Pharisees and his identification with the poor, or St. Paul's intrusion into the business practices of the silversmiths of Ephesus, without realizing the social responsibility of the people of God?

Dr. Norman's conception of the Christian task, with its cozy commitment to an exclusive interest in personal salvation and other-worldliness, ignores the tragedy of Christian ostrichism in time past. Where was the Orthodox Church of Russia when Bolshevism challenged the abuses of Czarism in Russia? Where was the Reformation church of Germany when Hitler and the Nazis took charge? Where was the Roman Catholic Church when Mussolini's fascist totalitarianism usurped authority in Italy? Somehow, the church had so defined its mission as to restrict itself from a major responsible role in the determination of those vital areas of the public and private life which ultimately determine the health of any national state or community of persons.

In one of his sermons, John Wesley declared:

> We . . . are the salt of the earth. . . . This is the reason why the providence of God has so mingled you together with other men that whatever grace you have received of God may through you be communicated to others; that every holy temper and word and work of yours may have an influence on them also. By this means a check, in some measure, be given to the corruption which is in the world; and a small part, at least, saved from the general infection.

The late Dr. Martin Luther King, Jr., more than any other American Christian leader, demonstrated the controversial crossfire which results when a Christian dares to confront the amoral practices of "the powers that be" in faithfulness to the gospel of Jesus Christ. He was a "born again" Christian who qualifies for high honors among those who, in the history of the church, have borne vicariously redemptive crosses. Dr. King brought deliverance to white and black people in the South who had been quarantined against each other by a *de jure/de facto* wall of separation.

Malachi Martin's series of articles on Pope Paul II reveals both incisive biography and impending prophecy. In pursuit of his Ph.D. degree, Pope John Paul II wrote a thesis on "The Phenomenology of Max Scheler." A quote from Scheler, according to Martin, offers a clue to the impending papacy of the new leader of Roman Catholicism: "If you succeed in taking a sense of the tragic from man and make him totally dependent on being happy, you have made him your slave." Scheler saw the heretical implications of a no-risk kind of Christianity, blissfully pursuing a self-protective piety while avoiding the redemptive, self-sacrificing requirements of the cross. Pope John Paul II may prove to be a strong advocate of just causes as well as a rugged defender of traditional Christianity.

The theology of church growth must be kept continually under review. In a recent article documenting the strategy of church growth employed by one denomination, it was refreshing to review an up-to-date methodology. One sensational result of its scientific procedures culminated in the opening of three new churches in the same city on the same Sunday. But the pragmatics of church growth reflected by the executive director is cause for reflection. He says that his denomination was "looking for the church type—a well-paid, well-educated family." Now, every kind of neighborhood deserves a church, but if Christian denominations selectively choose one kind of neighborhood and ignore other types, in the name of success pragmatics, race or class considerations, or the fiscal viability of potential constituents, God may have some misgivings about these so-called successes.

The remarkable changes taking place in the racial and cultural composition of this nation deserve the first consideration of *the church* and the churches. In 1955, for example, 89 percent of the immigrants entering the United States came from Europe; only 11 percent arrived from Africa, Latin America, and Asia. But in 1976, only 21 percent of America's immigrants came from Europe; 79 percent, came from Latin America, Asia, and Africa. America's color spectrum is deepening. Thirty percent of all of the immigrants who entered this nation in the last decade came from Latin America, Asia, and Africa. Beyond the year 2000, at present growth rates, approximately one-third of the American people will be non-white.

Dr. Tetsunao Yamamori's estimates of America's present ethinic constituency should make us pause:

> White Ethnics............................ 44 million
> African Americans..................... 25 million
> Native Americans...................... 800,000
> Hispanics................................. 19 million
> Japanese.................................. 951,000
> Chinese................................... 540,000
> Filipinos.................................. 350,000

His figures for non-white ethnics total almost 47 million.

The practical requirements of America's international diplomacy are forcing a liberalization of immigration policies in order to cultivate a positive rapport with nations of the Third World who heretofore were kept under rigid restrictions. It follows, therefore, that a principal church growth opportunity lies in this emerging pigmented section of the population. Furthermore, the importance of the African American sector of American Christianity must not be taken for granted. This constituency makes up 20 percent of the strength of U.S. Protestantism.

Net increases in the visible church come by one basic response: "professions of faith" in Christ. Transfers between churches or denominations represent simply the movement of the faithful. And much of the flag-waving over allegedly growing conservative churches represents simply the shifting loyalty of the discontented.

In 1949, for example, United Methodists received 400,000 persons on profession of faith. In 1977, that figure fell to 210,000. This represents 13.6 percent per thousand members. In 1959, the percentage was 18.24 percent per thousand members. Altar calls, church school, personal witnessing, and confirmation classes constitute the principal confession of faith channels. Seventy-five percent of the persons United Methodists received on profession of faith in 1977 were between the ages of ten and fourteen. Six out of ten of these persons came by way of the church school and the confirmation classes. One thing is clear—churches with strong Sunday schools and a multiplicity of small study groups and classes have a higher member retention rate than those with strong morning worship services and relatively weak Christian education programs.

Church membership losses are due to three basic causes: (1) death, (2) transfer, (3) the official dropping of inactive members. The death rate is almost beyond the control of any local church, though we do have a ministry which encourages health habits and tends to prolong the duration of life. Most churches transfer far more people in from other churches than those who transfer out. But the pernicious problem is the dropout rate which takes so-called inactive persons off membership rolls. If this dropout rate in the next ten years could be reduced by one-half and the present growth rate in the churches remained steady, membership increases in American churches would be phenomenal.

But it must be acknowledged that we have a "profession-of-faith" problem. In one denominational survey 14,234 churches (36.87 percent) reported not one new member on profession of faith; 25,431 (65.7 percent) reported less than four persons received on profession of faith. Eighty-three churches with over 500 members did not report one person on profession of faith; 22,674 churches (58.5 percent) indicated they had no confirmation classes; 750 of those churches had more than 500 members. It is clear that the churches must become more seriously engaged in carrying out the commission of Christ.

The good news, which may alter the predictions of the prophets of doom, is that there is a growing interest in evangelism in the life of the churches. Young child-bearing adults are beginning to recognize the indispensable role of the church in the lives of growing children and are returning to the church for Christian nurture. Small groups and short-term classes are increasing in number. Effective evangelism must be indivisibly linked with *ministry* (Christian nurture, education, and fellowship) for the growth and development of the people of God.

Some Christians want to sit and watch the sky and wait for the "second coming." That glorious hope must always be a lively prospect in the life of the church. The notion of the ultimate triumph of righteousness is deeply rooted in the ethos and expectation of Christianity. There are some totally committed to personal piety who spend their lives polishing their halos. Still others see the procurement of new converts as a statistical victory which is an end in itself. Others are committed to a life of prayer and hardly lift a hand to make the touch of Christ relevant to the stubborn justice issues and sinful habits in the world. But no one of these alternatives, if chosen, is according to divine instruction.

Jesus said, yea, commanded us, to go . . . teach . . . baptize . . . and do . . . all of the things he taught and demonstrated. Like John the Baptist of old, through our obedience we "prepare the way of the Lord." There is no time to waste. We must move!